ATHLETE'S
GUIDE TO
CAREER PLANNING

Al Petitpas, EdD
Springfield College

Delight Champagne, PhD
Springfield College

Judy Chartrand, PhD
Consulting Psychologists Press

Steven Danish, PhD
Virginia Commonwealth University

Shane Murphy, PhD
Gold Medal Consultants

Human Kinetics

Library of Congress Cataloging-in-Publication Data

Athlete's guide to career planning / Albert J. Petitpas . . . [et al.].
   p.   cm.
   Includes bibliographical references and index.
   ISBN 0-87322-459-0
   1. Athletics--Vocational guidance--United States.   2. Athletes-
-United States.   3. Career changes--United States.   I. Petitpas,
Albert J., 1947-   .
   GV706.8.A898   1997
   796'.023--DC20   96-46543
                                                          CIP

ISBN: 0-87322-459-0

Development Editors: Rodd Whelpley and Kent Reel; **Assistant Editor:** Jennifer Stallard; **Editorial Assistant:** Jennifer Hemphill; **Copyeditor:** Bob Replinger; **Proofreader:** Kathy Bennett; **Indexer:** Joan Griffitts; **Graphic Designer:** Robert Reuther; **Graphic Artist:** Kathy Boudreau-Fuoss; **Cover Designer:** Jack Davis; **Printer:** United Graphics

Human Kinetics books are available at special discounts for bulk purchase. Special editions or book excerpts can also be created to specification. For details, contact the Special Sales Manager at Human Kinetics.

Printed in the United States of America   10   9   8   7   6   5   4   3   2   1

Human Kinetics
Web site: http://www.humankinetics.com/

United States: Human Kinetics, P.O. Box 5076, Champaign, IL 61825-5076
1-800-747-4457
e-mail: humank@hkusa.com

Canada: Human Kinetics, Box 24040, Windsor, ON N8Y 4Y9
1-800-465-7301 (in Canada only)
e-mail: humank@hkcanada.com

Europe: Human Kinetics, P.O. Box IW14, Leeds LS16 6TR, United Kingdom
(44) 1132 781708
e-mail: humank@hkeurope.com

Australia: Human Kinetics, 57A Price Avenue, Lower Mitcham, South Australia 5062
(08) 277 1555
e-mail: humank@hkaustralia.com

New Zealand: Human Kinetics, P.O. Box 105-231, Auckland 1
(09) 523 3462
e-mail: humank@hknewz.com

Contents

Preface

Perennial NBA all-star Charles Barkley begins his introduction to the book *Hoop Dreams* by saying, "I know you won't believe me when I say this, but I wish kids, especially black kids, didn't dream so much about playing in the NBA. . . .** There are so many guys I know who had the intelligence to do almost anything, but all they thought about was basketball. And then when basketball didn't work out, they had nothing to turn to."

This may seem like a strange statement coming from a star athlete who is revered and emulated by countless young people throughout the world. However, we believe that Barkley has clearly described one of the critical challenges facing most athletes. Namely, to be successful in sport, you need to devote enormous amounts of time and energy to perfecting your athletic skills. If these efforts come at the expense of education or preparation for other life activities, then you too may have nothing to turn to when your sport career ends.

Over the years, we've worked with numerous high school, college, elite-amateur, and professional athletes. Many, like those Barkley described, didn't benefit from their sport experiences. These athletes enjoyed much success in sport—some even played professionally—but none were prepared to deal with their retirement from sport nor were they prepared to pursue a new career.

On the other hand, we've worked with many athletes who were very successful not only at playing their sport but also in learning important life skills from participation in it. These people viewed themselves not just as talented athletes but also as talented people. They have parlayed their sport success into life success. We've learned much from these athletes, and we wrote this book to help you learn their formula for success.

Our goal is to help athletes, from all levels of participation, realize the maximum benefit from their sport participation. Sport can be a dual-edged sword. On one side, sport can provide you with numerous opportunities to learn about yourself and others. On the other side, an exclusive commitment to sport can dominate your life so much that you won't be prepared for any other activity.

As you read through each chapter of this book, you'll learn how to prepare for each stage in your athletic career. Whether you're entering high school or retiring from professional sport, you'll find helpful hints on what to expect and how to grow through the experience.

Throughout the book, you'll read case studies of athletes we've worked with over the years. To protect their privacy we haven't used their real names. The stories, however, are true and illustrate much about athletic life and transitions. We've found that most athletes are accustomed to learning new skills and strategies by actively doing them, not just by observing. Therefore, we've provided numerous worksheets throughout the book for you to complete. These exercises will help you understand the material better and get you more actively involved in the learning process.

We've designed this book to help you learn the skills you need to plan effectively for future decisions and future careers. To accomplish this goal, we've divided the book into three sections. In the first section (chapters 1 through 4), we'll help you learn more about the transitions that you're likely to encounter during your athletic career and beyond. In chapter 1, we'll help you learn more about transitions. What typically happens to people during transitions? How do you handle difficult situations? How do you use your support systems? How do you plan for future events? In chapters 2 through 4, we've outlined some of the specific life tasks that you'll probably need to manage during high school, college, and elite or professional levels of competition.

In the second section (chapters 5 through 7), we'll help you learn more about yourself and the world of work. We'll also teach you the skills you need to have to reach your goals. In chapter 5, we guide you through a series of exercises to help you learn more about your values, needs, interests, and skills. This self-exploration will help you decide what things are most important to you. This information is critical if you're going to find a career that you'll truly enjoy. In chapter 6, we'll teach you how to identify careers that would best match your most important values, interests, and skills. In chapter 7, we'll teach you how to develop an action plan to accomplish your career goals.

In the third section of the book (chapters 8 through 10), we help you understand the career search process and teach you the skills and tools you'll need to get the career you want. In chapter 8, we give you some tips about job hunting in today's changing economy and teach you some job search strategies. In chapter 9, we'll show you how to write effective cover letters and resumes, and in chapter 10, we'll help you prepare for those all-important job interviews.

After you complete this book, you'll know a lot more about the types of transitions that you're likely to face. You'll have a better understanding of how to plan for future decisions and future careers. Chances are good that the more effort you put into completing the exercises in this book, the better prepared you'll be to effectively manage your career and life decisions.

Introduction

Career and Life Planning

In many ways, sport is your first career. As you read that sentence you were probably saying to yourself, "How can sport be my first career? I love to play sports. It's not work." Well, many people who have careers enjoy their jobs. These are people who found a career that matched their interests, needs, and skills. Others are unhappy with their jobs, and they work only because they need the money. Making enough money is clearly important, but a career must produce more than money before you can enjoy it in the same way that you enjoy playing your sport.

Some people have been lucky enough to just fall into the perfect job. But finding the right career need not depend solely on luck. This book will help you learn the skills you need to be able to find a career that's right for you. As you read through this book and complete the exercises in each chapter, you'll learn a new set of skills that will help you identify a satisfying career.

Actively searching for the right career, often called career planning, doesn't require magic. It uses the same process that you should use in making most decisions. To begin with, you need the right information. In

Career-Planning Process Phase I

Self-exploration — Career exploration — Career acquisition

career planning you need information in three main areas. First, you need to know a little about yourself. What do you need? What do you like? What interests you? What are your values, skills, and personality characteristics? We call this process *self-exploration.*

The next step is to discover your possible options. Which careers would best fit your values, needs, interests, skills, and personality? Are employers hiring people for these jobs? What training or education do you need to prepare for these jobs? This step in the career process is called *career exploration.*

After you know what you would like to do, then you need to learn how to land a job in the field you've chosen. How do you find where the jobs are? How do you get an interview or write a resume? These skills are what you learn in the third phase of the career development process—*career acquisition.* By gathering the types of information you need to make a good career choice, you accomplish the first phase of the career-planning process. This diagram is shown at the top of the page.

MAKING GOOD DECISIONS

Career development is a process of making good decisions. You're more likely to make good decisions when you have the right information. Unfortunately many people make decisions about their careers without the right information. For example, a person may choose to major in history in college solely because he liked history in high school, or an individual may want to be an accountant only because her mother is an accountant. Although these choices may work out well, people who make decisions without first examining their needs and the options available to them run the risk of locking themselves into careers in which they aren't happy or satisfied.

Many people have made important decisions about their lives and careers without having enough information. Think about all the things that you bought over the years that you soon wished you hadn't bought. More information might have led to better decisions and more satisfaction in the long run. The same is true with finding a career. Better information usually leads to better decisions.

Let's examine a case where an athlete didn't take the time for self-exploration or career exploration.

Guy is a two-time college all-American hockey player. A National Hockey League franchise drafted him and assigned him to a high-level farm club. Guy had a very successful first year in professional hockey and seemed headed for the parent club when he suffered a freak injury that eventually ended his career. He tried several comebacks, but the injury so hampered his speed and cutting ability that he could never regain his level of play. Guy hung on for two years, but when the club didn't extend his contract, he found himself out of professional sport.

Guy had known that his career would someday end, but he hadn't anticipated that he would be looking for a new career at age 26. Fortunately, Guy had taken a couple of courses during his off-seasons and had earned enough credits to graduate with a degree in social science.

For the first time in his life Guy didn't know what he was going to do. He applied for a couple of high school coaching jobs but quickly realized that he couldn't live on the three or four thousand dollars that these positions offered. He thought about teaching, but he didn't take the certification courses or do the practice teaching necessary to be eligible. He found himself without a sense of direction.

Finally, a friend suggested that Guy talk to a local politician whom they both knew through hockey. Guy was reluctant at first but soon made the call, which led to a position as a social worker. Guy's new job was to assist the courts in custody cases. He interviewed parents and children in families that were going through divorce and made recommendations to the judge about custody of the children after the marriage ended.

At first the job seemed OK, but Guy didn't like always ending up the bad guy. No matter what he did, he felt that the parents and children saw him as the enemy, the person who was breaking up their

> *family. This situation was a long way from his years in hockey when he'd been a crowd favorite because of his flashy play. Guy never realized how important it was for him to feel that people liked him. He couldn't take the stress and bad feelings, so after three months he quit.*
>
> *Guy fell into a few other jobs through contacts with friends, but none lasted longer than a few months. Guy was finding it a tough adjustment to go from star to bottom of the totem pole. Now, at 28 years of age, Guy felt like a loser.*

In many ways Guy's problems developed because he was trying to make a major life decision without the right information. Guy is still not clear about his values, needs, interests, and skills. He could luck out and fall into the right position, but this doesn't often happen. Instead of taking the time for self-exploration and career exploration, Guy is relying on a fishing approach to finding a career. He keeps casting out into the ocean hoping to catch a big fish without knowing what is out there or what kind of bait to use. Chances are that Guy will continue to miss the right career until he learns what to look for.

Guy's story illustrates a fact of life for most athletes, namely that sport careers often end relatively early in life. It's rare to see professional baseball, basketball, football, or hockey players who still compete after age 35. For female athletes, the end of a sport career may come even sooner because there are fewer professional opportunities for women.

Guy knew that his sport career would eventually end, but he wasn't prepared for it to end while he was in his mid-20s. He thought that working outside his sport was a long way off, so he hadn't made plans for the changes and choices he was having to make.

Part of career development is conducting self-exploration and career exploration and learning the skills to find the right career. The other part of career development is planning for future changes or transitions.

All athletes go through *transitions*. Moving from high school to college athletics or from junior- to senior-levels of competition are examples of *normal sport transitions*. But athletes must sometimes deal with *unexpected transitions*, like the one forced upon Guy when injury ended his playing career. Part of effective career planning is learning to anticipate normal transitions and learning how to use your skills and resources to cope with unplanned transitions. If you add planning for transitions to the process you use to make good decisions, then your career-planning process expands to look like the diagram at the top of the next page.

Career-Planning Process
Phases I & II

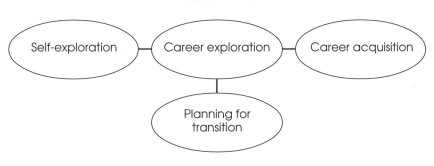

If you have the right information and you've planned for the expected and unexpected transitions in your life, you still need a game plan to get the right career. The final part of the career-planning process is developing a goal-setting plan to achieve your career goals. The purpose of having an action plan is to give you a sense of direction and help you anticipate and cope with any roadblocks that may get in the way of your career planning. The action plan puts your information and skills together in a

Career-Planning Process
Phases I, II, & III

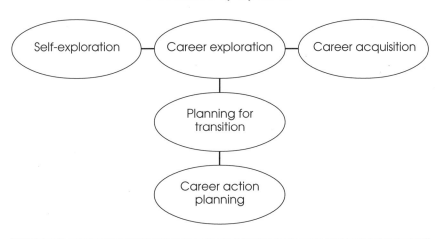

way that will enable you to get the right career. If you add a career action plan to your career-planning process, your final model of career planning would look like the diagram at the bottom of page xiii.

Even though you may have already graduated from high school or college, we suggest that you read chapters 2 and 3 to get a sense of how you may have made some of your earlier decisions. You can use this book on your own or with others. In either case, it's helpful to share this information with friends and family. People who know you well can often help you understand yourself better. We'll show you how others can help when we look at the support people in your life as part of our exercises on managing transitions in chapter 1.

LOOKING AHEAD

As you read through the chapters and complete the exercises, you'll be learning a set of skills that you'll be able to use throughout your life. Most people have at least three careers in their lifetimes. A career is different from a job. A career is a series of jobs that you undertake in a planned effort to achieve your personal goals. A job is any particular paid position that you've held. Jobs can be related to your career or they can be unrelated. If sport is your first career, you'll probably have at least two more careers before you retire.

Learning how to do career planning will help you find careers that you truly enjoy. You may still need to be lucky, but we believe in the old saying "Luck is when preparation meets opportunity." If you complete the exercises in the following chapters, we believe that you'll be ready to take advantage of any career opportunities that present themselves to you.

PART I

Transitions in Life and Sport

Transitions

Everyone reaches points in life when major changes occur. These points are called *transitions.* As an athlete, you may have already gone through a few transitions—for example, moving from high school to college sport or from junior- to senior-level competition. Some of the changes that you have to make are physical (putting on more weight or adding strength), and some are psychological or emotional (accepting a lack of playing time).

UNDERSTANDING TRANSITIONS

Sometimes the psychological aspects of a transition can get in the way of an athlete's career progress. For example, some Olympic athletes experience confusion and sadness when the games are over or when they don't qualify for a competition. Recently, we've worked with a large number of athletes through a program sponsored by the United States Olympic Committee called the Career Assistance Program for Athletes (CAPA). During these meetings, we introduce Olympic-level athletes to the career-planning process through a workshop that covers the topics outlined in the introduction of this book. Some of the athletes have retired from elite-level sport. Others are considering retirement, and the remainder are still competing but want to get a head start on their career planning. As part of these workshops, athletes have an opportunity to share their feelings about retirement from sport. Those who have retired or are in the process of considering retirement have shared many concerns.

A track-and-field athlete who had been a college all-American and a national champion told us what it was like when he didn't make the 1992 Olympic team. "I feel so alone. Nobody understands what I am going through. Everyone is telling me how proud I should feel because I made it to the Olympic trials, but they don't know how it hurts inside to not go to Barcelona." Although he believed that people were trying to be helpful to him, he still felt as though no one really understood what he was feeling.

Another Olympic nonqualifier reinforced the importance of sport in the life of elite athletes. She talked about what it felt like when she feared that her competitive career was over. "Swimming was my whole life. Nothing is going to give me the high that I got after a great race. My life feels empty, just like I was in a great big hole with no way out." A member of the baseball team described similar feelings. "I was always introduced to people as a baseball player, now that it's over I don't know who I am. Maybe I could go back to school, but it's not going to be like playing ball."

A member of the U.S. ski team reminded us that retirement from sport involves more than just not competing. "It's not just skiing that I miss, it's everything about it. I am losing my teammates, the travel, the celebrations. Everything is going to be different."

In these four examples the athletes were feeling badly about the loss of sport in their lives. They had not given much thought to life without sport until they were forced to retire. This transition affected their self-identity, their support systems, and their lifestyles. Not all transitions in your athletic life cycle will be as tumultuous as retirement from sport, but each requires a certain degree of physical and psychological adjustment.

Predictable Transitions

Many of the transitions that you have to manage are *predictable*. Each sport has a life cycle of expected levels of competition and age of retirement. For example, some of the predictable transitions in the sport life cycle of a professional basketball player are the following: town team ->junior high team -> high school junior varsity -> high school varsity -> college -> professional -> retirement.

The sport life cycle for a professional basketball player begins at about age 10 when the athlete begins to learn how to play and ends with retirement at about age 35. In 25 years of playing basketball, a professional athlete can expect at least seven normal transitions. Let's look at some of the transitions that one basketball player experienced.

William's Story

William began playing basketball when he was 10 years old. He and several friends joined an instructional league that was just forming in the section of the city where he lived. Although William had never played basketball before, he quickly learned the game, and his height gave him an advantage over many of his teammates. During the next few years, William fell in love with the game. He practiced every day after school and played at a local Boys Club four nights a week. By the time he was 13, he was the most valuable player on a town team that reached the state finals. People in the community began to associate him with the sport.

There were two public and six parochial high schools in town, and William decided to attend a small Catholic school where most of his friends were going. He knew most of the guys on the basketball team from pickup games in the neighborhood, so he figured he would have no trouble fitting in. William was disappointed when he didn't make the varsity team as a freshman. He felt a little better when he learned that the coach had him playing junior varsity so he could get more playing time. By the third game of his sophomore year William was a starter on the varsity. He was voted all-league his junior year and most valuable player in the league his senior year.

Besides adjusting to basketball, William had to adapt to the academic demands of high school. William was an average student, but the desire to remain eligible forced him to hit the books. These efforts resulted in a solid B average and earned William the Scholar Athlete Award for his city. William's parents didn't know very much about basketball, but they enjoyed watching him compete and were very proud of his academic accomplishments. Basketball had become a major part of William's life and identity. During his senior year in high school, a small number of college basketball programs recruited him. Unfortunately, William's parents didn't know much about colleges in general, and they knew even less about college athletics. William and his parents had to decide if he should take a partial scholarship to a Division I school with the agreement that he would be given a "full ride" if he proved to be a solid contributor to the team, or if he should go to a Division II school with all expenses paid. To confuse matters even more, an Ivy League school was very interested in William, but they wanted him to go to a prep school for a year or two to further develop his academic and athletic skills. William's parents left the decision up to him.

Eventually William decided to go to the Division I college. He figured that the scholarship money he received as Scholar Athlete, coupled with the partial tuition grant, would pay for his first year in school. When official practice began, William wondered if he had made the right decision. He was the third shooting guard on the team and rarely got any court time. To make matters worse, another highly touted shooting guard committed to the college during the early signing period. William went through a period of about three weeks when he had little energy for school or basketball. He felt down and his confidence was at an all-time low.

Shortly after the basketball season ended, William visited a high school friend who was attending a small Division III school. By chance, he was introduced to the dean of the college, who happened to be a basketball fan and remembered William from high school. After much thought and a few more difficult experiences at his Division I college, William decided to transfer to the smaller school. He ended up having a very successful basketball career, leading the team in scoring and assists for two years. William received regional all-American honorable mention and graduated with his class as a solid B student. He majored in psychology during his college years because he liked the introductory course but never gave much thought to what he might do with this major later on.

After graduation, William felt lost. He had always gone to school because he wanted to play basketball, but now he had to get a real job. He spent the next six months working as a substitute teacher, but he disliked all the discipline problems and felt empty inside. Finally, William realized that his basketball career was over and that he had to get on with his life. At 22 years of age, William was just beginning to ask himself who he was other than a basketball player.

William's story isn't unusual. He was an exceptional athlete who enjoyed a successful athletic career. Yet William had to make a number of adjustments. The transitions into high school and college, his decision to transfer, and his adjustment to life without basketball were all major events in William's life. What was left out of this story is how William coped with each of the transitions. William used some of his own skills in coping with these changes in his life, but he also used support from others.

Unexpected Transitions

While reading this story, you may have noticed that some of the transitions in William's life were predictable. Leaving high school is a predictable transition. Besides predictable transitions, a number of *unexpected* changes can occur. For example, thousands of athletes like William plan to be professional basketball players, but only a few hundred play in the NBA each year. The average career in the NBA is about three years, so most basketball players are forced to retire from their sport before they had planned. At each level of the basketball life cycle there are fewer and fewer players. Teams fail to select them, they become injured, or they choose to retire. Do you remember Guy, the hockey player you read about in the introduction? Guy was one of a few special players to make it to professional hockey, but his career ended when he was 26 years of age. William's career ended at 22. Women have even fewer opportunities at the professional level, so most of their careers end while they are in their 20s.

Sometimes a transition occurs because a change that you are expecting doesn't take place. These transitions are called *nonevents*. For example, as a junior in high school you might expect to move up to the varsity team. If your coach keeps you on the junior varsity, you might become discouraged or angry and quit the team. William thought he was going to play high school varsity as a freshman. When they didn't move him up from the JV team, he felt down.

Understanding the way that transitions affect us and planning for future transitions are important parts of our career planning. Let's begin by looking at your sport's life cycle and some of the unexpected transitions that may occur. To begin, complete worksheets 1.1 and 1.2.

Examining Your Sport Life Cycle

If you look back at your sport life cycle, you may be surprised to see that your sport career is not as long as your work career or that your sport career and work career overlap. Many athletes have been able to adjust to their transition out of sport by learning about or working in another career while still competing. Two examples of this are professional athletes who get career experience during the off-season and Olympic athletes who work for companies as part of the Olympic Jobs Opportunity Program while training for competitions. By gaining work experience, these

Worksheet 1.1:

Your Sport Life Cycle

Life cycles vary among sports. For example, gymnasts usually begin to learn different events by age 8 and retire in their 20s, while golfers might not begin to play until their teen years but can play into their 60s and beyond. An important part of career planning is preparing for transitions. By answering the following questions, you'll begin to examine your sport life cycle.

1. How old were you when you started playing your sport?

2. How did you get interested in playing your sport?

3. Who taught you how to play?

4. How did your parents or guardians feel about your playing your sport?

5. What was the first transition you had to make and how did it affect your feelings and behaviors?

6. What other transitions can you expect?

7. Does your sport have a professional league? If yes, do you feel that you have the ability and desire to play at the professional level?

8. How old do you think you'll be when you begin your first nonsport career?

9. How many years do you think that you'll be playing your sport?

10. How many years do you think you'll be spending in your new work career?

Other Transitions—Some Questions to Ask Yourself

Now let's see if you've gone through any other types of transitions.

1. What transitions do you expect to go through in the next few years?

2. Has there ever been an event in your life that you didn't expect, such as an injury that caused you to go through an unexpected transition? If yes, describe what happened and how it affected you.

3. What other transitions might occur that would be unexpected, unwanted, or unlikely?

4. Have you ever expected an event to occur (such as making a team or qualifying for an event) that didn't happen? If yes, what happened and how did you react?

5. Have any events happened outside your sport (such as a family illness) that affected your play?

---

athletes are able to get a taste of the world of work and gain additional information about their likes and dislikes. Even if you're a high school student, it isn't too early to start planning for future careers. The earlier you start gathering information about yourself and the world of work, the better your career choices are likely to be.

Doing career planning while you're still competing offers several advantages. First, as you learn more about career planning you'll gain more confidence in your ability to gain a satisfying career. This confidence may even help you perform better in your sport. For example, in 1986 about 35 women who were competing on the Ladies Professional Golf Association tour participated in a program called Planning for Future Careers. These athletes included both tour rookies and long-time veterans. Although the focus of the program was to help the athletes prepare for their eventual retirement by teaching them about career planning, several commented that they gained more confidence not only about their ability to find a new career but also in themselves. One veteran player described it as follows:

> I can't tell you how different I feel about things now. For the last couple of years I felt that I was just hanging on. I was not thinking about winning tournaments. I just hoped I could make the cut each week. I would get over a three- or four-foot putt and tell myself that if I choked my whole career would be over. I can't tell you how much pressure I put on myself. I know I was becoming my own worst enemy but golf was all I knew how to do and I could not imagine my life without it. Now I feel as though I learned a lot of skills throughout my golf career and I feel so much better about my future. I now feel confident that I will find another career that I will enjoy. The funny thing is that the three footers don't seem quite as long and I'm making more putts. I think that I am just more relaxed about my future and it's helping my game now.

A second advantage of doing career planning while you're still competing is that it gives you a sense of direction after you retire from your sport. Many athletes who we've spoken to said that when they were forced to retire from their sport they felt lost. So much of their lives was tied up in being athletes that they had difficulty seeing themselves doing anything else. Through the process of career planning, you begin to see the many roles that you play. You also begin to understand that what you learn in sport may transfer into other areas of your life. Career planning gives you a road map to the future so you won't feel lost.

Another advantage of career planning is that it helps you learn more about yourself. This self-knowledge can help you not only in finding a new career but also in improving your academic and social life. Outside distractions can affect our sport performance. If you've just had a fight with a family member or close friend, you may have difficulty getting your focus back to the point where you can perform at your best. Career planning helps you identify skills that enable you to better handle family, school, or social problems.

Examining your sport life cycle helps you prepare for transitions. By starting your career planning while you're still competing, you identify the skills and support resources that help you cope with transitions and prepare for the future. Let's look at some of the skills you may have used in coping with your transitions.

COPING WITH TRANSITIONS

As you looked at the transitions that you've gone through, you probably remembered how you reacted in each situation. Many of the things that you did to cope with your situation were probably helpful, but you may have also done some things that got in the way of working through the transition. For some examples, let's look at Beth, a promising 17-year-old high school soccer player.

Beth's Story

Beth was a two-time all-state performer who had already accepted a full athletic scholarship to a major college soccer powerhouse. During the winter months, Beth was a starter on the varsity basketball team. During the third game of the season she severely injured her right knee diving for a loose ball. The injury required surgery to repair torn ligaments, and the doctors told Beth that with hard work she would be as good as new in a few months.

This was Beth's first major injury. She was afraid, and she was angry at herself for getting injured because she felt it was a stupid play on her part. She also felt that she had let her parents and friends down because of what might happen if she didn't fully recover. She asked herself many of the same questions she heard her friends asking: Would she lose her scholarship? Would she be able to play as well as before? Did she make a mistake by playing basketball this year?

Up to this point, it seemed that the anger, guilt, and other feelings that resulted from the injury caused Beth to doubt herself and her ability to cope with the situation. She found it easier to be alone than to deal with family and friends. Although withdrawing from people brought her temporary relief from her feelings, it also kept her away from the support she needed to get through this unexpected transition.

During her rehabilitation, Beth refused to go to basketball games or social events that she normally attended. She was very moody and seemed to become angry at the smallest thing. Her boyfriend would come over to visit, but these meetings usually ended in a fight because Beth would say he didn't know what she was going through. She was becoming frustrated at her progress in physical therapy, even though she was reaching her therapist's treatment goals. She would be particularly demanding of her therapist if her strength or range of motion had not improved from day to day. Her frustration led her to ignore her therapist's recommendations. She pushed her exercises so hard that she cried from the pain and then became angry at herself for not being tough enough. Instead of getting better, Beth suffered a setback.

Although Beth was trying to deal with her feelings, she found herself pushing away the people who were trying to help her. At the same time her fear caused her to make some poor decisions about her rehabilitation program. Fortunately, Beth was able to get the support she needed to work through her feelings.

Beth's physical therapist introduced her to a counselor who was working in the training room. The counselor listened to Beth's story and tried to understand what she was going though. For the first time Beth was able to voice her anger and sadness. After this, the counselor helped Beth identify the skills that she had used to become a good athlete and showed her how to use them to deal with her injury. Beth had not been prepared for her injury, and her emotions kept her from using the goal-setting and imagery techniques that she used to improve her sport skills.

Beth had also failed to seek help from others. Before her injury, she had always sought out the best coaches for advice and had often talked with players she admired to learn more about game strategies and techniques. She withdrew from this type of support while she was injured. Once Beth learned to use her skills and the support of others, she made better decisions about her rehabilitation and made a quick recovery.

Beth's case illustrates the importance of dealing with transitions. At first Beth was unable to manage her emotional reaction to her injury. Instead of using her normal style of solving problems, she kept her emotions bottled up and avoided her family and friends. The surprise of her unexpected injury found her unprepared to cope with the changes that were occurring. The fear of losing her sport and her guilt over letting her parents and friends down caused her to make bad decisions. With the help of a counselor, Beth was able to express her feelings and get back to using her skills.

By preparing for transitions as part of your career planning, you can avoid some of the down time that Beth experienced. Remember that Beth was able to get back on track by using her own problem-solving skills and the support of others.

Identifying Your Coping Skills

In preparing for transitions, you need to examine both your coping skills and your support resources. Let's begin by looking at how Beth coped with her injury. Beth did some things that got in the way of her recovery. For example, she had trouble talking about her feelings. She let her anger and guilt get in the way of her rehabilitation. She withdrew from her family, teammates, and friends. She didn't use the support of her physical therapist. Let's call these *problem behaviors*. She also did some things that helped her recover, such as using goal setting and imagery, and sharing her feelings with the counselor. These we'll call *positive behaviors*. Beth's behaviors in managing her injury are outlined in highlight box 1.1.

Highlight Box 1.1

How Beth Coped With Her Injury

Problem behaviors
1. Beth didn't share her feelings with her support team.
2. Beth withdrew from her family and friends.
3. Beth didn't follow the advice of her physical therapist.
4. Beth let her feelings control her life.
5. Beth didn't seek out the advice of other athletes who had coped with similar injuries.

Positive behaviors
1. Beth was able to use her counselor as a sounding board to vent some of her feelings.
2. Beth was able to use goal setting and imagery during her rehabilitation.
3. Beth was able to reconnect with her support team and use their assistance.
4. Beth was a hard worker, and once she made better decisions about her rehabilitation she improved quickly.

By completing worksheets 1.3 and 1.4, you can examine your style of handling difficult situations. You'll be using this information later in the chapter when you develop your game plan for managing transitions.

Building a Support Team for Transitions

Although most of us would like to be independent, we all come to recognize that we need other people to get us through difficult or uncertain times. As an athlete, you may have learned how to endure pressure and bad times by sucking it up or giving 110 percent. You may have been taught that asking for help is a sign of weakness and that any

Worksheet 1.3:

How Do You Cope With Transitions?

Think back to the transitions that you've already gone through during your sport career. Using the case of Beth as an example, identify problem behaviors and positive behaviors that you used.

A. List any problem behaviors or positive behaviors that you've used during transitions.

Problem behaviors	*Positive behaviors*
1. _____	1. _____
2. _____	2. _____
3. _____	3. _____
4. _____	4. _____
5. _____	5. _____

B. Remember that the positive skills that you used in coping with a transition can help you in dealing with new transitions. The key is to eliminate the problem behaviors and increase the positive behaviors. What positive behaviors can you use to grow through your next transition? (If you're having difficulty coming up with these behaviors, move to the next exercise on identifying coping skills.)

C. Besides the positive behaviors that you've already used, future transitions may require new behaviors. What new positive behaviors can you list that may help you in coping with future transitions?

Worksheet 1.4:

Identifying Your Coping Skills

You probably have developed a number of other skills that you could use in dealing with transitions. Many of the skills that you've learned to be successful in sports can also be helpful in other areas of your life. Use the following exercise to help you identify some of these skills.

A. What do you do to prepare for a major competition? List those techniques that you use to prepare physically and those that you use to prepare mentally.

Physical

1. _____
2. _____
3. _____
4. _____
5. _____
6. _____
7. _____
8. _____
9. _____
10. _____

Mental

1. _____
2. _____
3. _____
4. _____
5. _____
6. _____
7. _____
8. _____
9. _____
10. _____

B. Place a circle around any of the physical or mental techniques that you use to prepare for a major competition that you could also use in coping with a transition. For example, if you had listed "Read the scouting report on the competition" as a mental skill and you're preparing to move from high school to college sports, you could use the same strategy to find out as much as you could about the college you're planning to attend. Remember, the more information you have, the better choices you're likely to make and the fewer surprises you're likely to meet.

sign of weakness can make you vulnerable and allow your opponent to gain an advantage.

Seeking the support of others is neither a sign of dependency nor a sign of weakness. It's a sign that you know that others may have the information, strength, or knowledge that you don't have in a given area of your life. If you think for a moment about teamwork, you may understand better why support is necessary. On soccer teams, for example, forwards and sweepers play different positions because they have different strengths as players. A team relies on the forwards to provide the scoring, while the sweeper's primary job is to disrupt the other team's offensive charges and to protect the goalie. It's very rare when one player on a team has all the skills necessary to win a game alone. Each player relies on the strengths of others to improve team play.

In a similar way, everyone needs a team of people who can help in life. You can't win all the time if you rely only on yourself. Even athletes who play individual sports like figure skating or archery have a team of people who prepare them for competitions and support them during training. Coaches, trainers, parents, family members, and other athletes can all contribute to the success of an individual-sport athlete. These people may provide information, motivation, skills training, emotional support, criticism, and even money to help an athlete achieve his or her goals. As an athlete, you've probably served as a support person for team members, younger athletes, or friends.

Support teams in the world outside sport can look quite similar to the one you may have developed for yourself in your athletic career. In the section that follows you'll have an opportunity to examine your existing support team to see if it will help you cope with transitions in your sport, your career, and your life.

Your Support Team

Whether you're making a career choice, striving for a sport award, or trying to do well at school, you always need the support of others. Support or help that people can give you or that you can give others comes in various forms. A person's support team is made up of different types of people. If you read the descriptions of the types of people in figure 1.1, you may recognize some people on your support team.

Now let's take a better look at the support people on your team. In reading the descriptions below, you may notice that some people in your life play more than one support role. Your coach, for example, may be a

Your Support Team

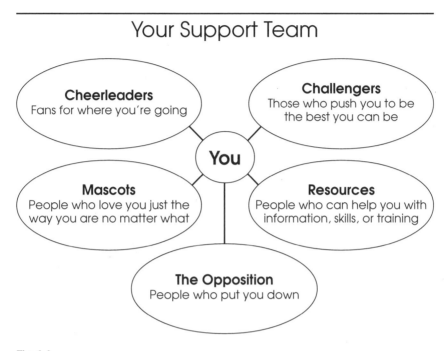

Fig. 1.1.

cheerleader sometimes, a challenger most of the time, and even an opponent at other times.

- Cheerleaders are the fans for where you're going. Everyone needs cheerleaders, both on and off the playing field. You need people to cheer you on in your career plans and efforts.

- Challengers are people who push you to reach your greatest potential. These people often make you work harder, think harder, and try harder than you ever thought you could. In choosing and striving for a career, you'll need people who can help you dream about your future outside sport.

- Mascots are people who love us just the way we are. A mascot is someone who accepts you when you fail and hugs you when you're down. Sometimes mascots won't challenge you because they don't want to hurt your feelings. Mascots are wonderful when you're looking for jobs and you haven't been as successful as you had hoped.

- Resource people help us by providing information, training, or advice. Counselors, teachers, friends, coaches, librarians, neighbors, or relatives might be good resources for athletes who are making career decisions.

- The Opposition says negative things to us about our performance or abilities. They're always looking for our weak spots. They may make us question ourselves. They may say, "You'll never make it to the Olympics" or, "No one gets teaching jobs any more." They work against us when we try hard. Sometimes they motivate us by getting us to say, "I'll show him!"

Let's examine your support team. Complete worksheets 1.5 and 1.6.

Now that you've looked at your support team, you may want to think about the role that support plays in your life right now and what it may mean to you in future transitions. By examining your support world, you may have discovered that you've been relying too heavily on some support team members. Perhaps you need to find new team members or strike out on your own. You may also have realized that people who hold certain support roles during one transition or time of life may be hindering you in a current transition. For example, your cheerleaders and mascots may have been great supports while you were playing your sport, but they may not be able to cushion you from the rejections or hard knocks you may meet during your job search. Likewise, your challengers may have been terrific in motivating you on the playing field, but they may become the opposition when you try to make career choices that take time and energy away from your sport career.

Like sports teams, your support team will need to change over time. A team member who was a star contributor one year may not perform as well when the situation or the rules change. Being aware of your changing needs can help you restructure your support team so that you can manage a particular transition. Additionally, it can help you identify areas in which you might like to become more independent of the influence and support of others.

Finally, after looking at your support team, you may have noticed that you are or can be a support team member for other people on and off the playing field. Your experience has enabled you to develop skills and knowledge that may be extremely helpful to others. Parents, coaches, friends, and other athletes may really need your help. Support is like the ocean tide; it ebbs and flows. By giving help to others you'll gain not only support but also the skills and confidence you need to manage transitions throughout life.

Worksheet 1.5:

Who Are the Support People in Your World?

List the names of the people in your support world under the type of support that they provide. Remember that one person can provide different types of support, so the same name might appear more than once.

Cheerleaders

1. _____
2. _____
3. _____
4. _____
5. _____
6. _____
7. _____
8. _____

Challengers

1. _____
2. _____
3. _____
4. _____
5. _____
6. _____
7. _____
8. _____

Mascots

1. _____
2. _____
3. _____
4. _____
5. _____
6. _____
7. _____
8. _____

Resources

1. _____
2. _____
3. _____
4. _____
5. _____
6. _____
7. _____
8. _____

The Opposition

1. _____
2. _____
3. _____
4. _____

5. _____
6. _____
7. _____
8. _____

Worksheet 1.6:

Some Final Questions to Ask Yourself About Your Support World

Look at your support world in Worksheet 1.6 and ask yourself the following questions about the picture of the support world that you see.

1. Who are the major support people in my life?

2. Do I rely on just one or two people to give me support, or do I have a large number of different support people?

3. Are all of the support people actually available to me most of the time?

4. Do all of these support people know each other?

5. Do I have many people providing only one type of support (such as cheerleaders), or do I have support people in each of the categories?

6. Which types of support are most helpful to me and which are least helpful?

7. Do I need more of a certain type of support to help me with a specific task or transition?

8. What can I do right now to fill in the gaps in my support world?

9. Who needs my support right now? How can I be helpful to them?

Worksheet 1.7:

Your Game Plan for Transitions

1. Identify a transition that may be coming up for you.

2. List your personal coping resources.

3. List the types of support that are available to you.

4. List any deficits in your personal coping resources or support team.

5. How will you get the skills or resources that you need?

6. How will this transition fit in with the overall plan you have for your life or career?

(Refer to later chapters on goal setting and career acquisition.)

PUTTING IT ALL TOGETHER

Preparing for transitions helps you develop the personal and support resources that you need not only to cope with changes but to actually grow through the experience. Success in managing change helps you build confidence in your abilities and assists you with future transitions. You've already gathered a lot of information about your transitions and resources by completing the worksheets in this chapter. Now you can put this new information about transitions to use by completing worksheet 1.7.

Now that you've completed your first game plan for transition, share it with other athletes who have already gone through a similar experience. If you can't identify someone, ask your coach or other members of your support team for some suggestions. By sharing this information, you'll be able to get some advice about your game plan. You may also discover new people to add to your support team or learn about other coping strategies you could use or other coping skills you could develop.

CHAPTER SUMMARY

Adjusting to the physical and emotional demands of transitions is an important part of career planning. As an athlete you have to deal with all the transitions that nonathletes have to deal with plus those changes specific to your sport.

From this chapter, you should have learned the following:

1. Transitions are points in your life when you have to make changes or adjustments.

2. Adjusting to the physical and emotional changes caused by transitions is an important part of your career planning.

3. Many of the transitions in your athletic life are predictable and expected.

4. Some transitions, like those caused by a serious injury, are unexpected.

5. A transition can also occur when an event that you expected to happen doesn't happen (a nonevent).

6. There are advantages to doing career planning while you're still playing your sport.

7. Coping with transitions requires that you identify and use life skills.

8. Support people are needed to cope with transitions.

Chapter 2

High School

High school years are often a time for fun and friendships, **but these years usually include many transitions for student-athletes.** Your academic achievements, career choices, and personal relationships often change or become much more important. In high school, the courses that you take and the grades that you achieve will often determine what careers you can seek or what colleges you can attend. Your relationships with others usually change. At times you feel like an adult, but your parents and teachers seem to treat you like a child. Adjusting to all the changes that can take place during the high school years can be difficult. Besides these changes, you'll face two major tasks during high school—learning about who you are and deciding whether to prepare for college or for your nonsport career. In this chapter, we'll give you some of the information that you need to make good decisions about these tasks.

DEFINING YOUR PERSONAL IDENTITY

For most people the high school years mark the beginning of a process of deciding who we are and how we define ourselves to the world. This process is called *identity development*. To help you understand what we mean, think about how you would describe yourself to a stranger. You may have thought, "I'm a gymnast" or, "I'm a soccer player." In giving yourself a label you've defined yourself as an athlete. You could have said, "I'm an honor role student" or, "I'm an artist." Some of the information that you use to define yourself comes from inside you and usually reflects things that you do well. You think of yourself as the best field hockey player in the school or the starting point guard on the basketball team. You feel good about your ability to do something well.

Another factor in developing your "label" is the reinforcement that comes from others. People begin to identify you with your skills. Even as a child you probably can remember people saying things about how high you could jump or how fast you could run. It doesn't take long before people begin to identify you with your skill area. You often hear people say something like "There's Mary, she's a great goaltender" or "Bob is the best skier in the region." These statements reinforce individuals' pictures of themselves. You can see how the combination of athletic skills and external reinforcements come into play in the identity development of one young figure skater.

Cathy was a 16-year-old high school sophomore and one of the most promising figure skaters in the United States. From a very early age, it was clear that she was a special skater. By age 8, she was doing jumps and moves at the local rink that most of the girls twice her age wouldn't even attempt. By junior high it was apparent that Cathy had the potential to become an elite-level figure skater.

Cathy's mother, a very good figure skater herself, recognized her daughter's talents from the beginning and obtained for her the best equipment and coaching that money could buy. When Cathy had gone as far as she could under the guidance of the local coaches, her parents decided to send her to live and train in Boston at a highly selective skating club. Cathy, who was 12 at the time, was hesitant to be away from her family and friends, but she knew that training with a world famous coach would help her reach her ultimate goal of winning an Olympic medal.

The skating club arranged for Cathy to stay with a Boston family that lived a short walk from the rink. Cathy would get up early every day to be at skating practice from 5:30 to 7:30 in the morning. She would go to school from 8:15 to 2:30 in the afternoon and then go back to practice from 4:00 to 6:30 in the evening. After dinner, Cathy would study for a few hours and usually go to bed before 10:00. On the weekends, Cathy would have five hours of practice each day. She had the rest of the weekend to herself.

Although Cathy's schedule was demanding and she missed her friends and family back home, she loved to skate and knew that this is what it would take to make nationals. The older skaters at the rink reassured her that all the hard work was necessary. They told Cathy she would always have time to meet boys and play with her friends, but she would never have another chance at winning a national championship or Olympic medal. Cathy made the commitment to be the best skater she could be. During the next four years, she quickly moved through the junior ranks. At 16 she was considered one of the brightest prospects in the United States.

As you can see, Cathy's life centered on skating. She identified herself as a skater and was willing to make whatever sacrifices were necessary to further her skating career.

Selecting a personal identity, like making a decision, is best done when you have the right information. The more you know about yourself and the world around you, the more capable you'll be in defining who you are. You learn about yourself by trying out different activities, playing different roles, and meeting different people. If all you do is participate in your sport, you may narrow how you define yourself before you know enough about your other values, needs, interests, and skills.

The problem with defining yourself as an athlete or a student is that you are only describing what you do—not who you are. The more you focus your energies in one area, the more vulnerable you are if anything happens that keeps you from participating in that activity. For example, if you feel confident in yourself only as an athlete and you experience a career-ending injury, your whole identity may be threatened. Let's revisit Cathy to see what can happen.

Success followed success for Cathy, but suddenly she began to struggle. She met her first major disappointment in an important regional competition when she fell twice and finished well below the top competitors. Saying that her poor performance was a wake-up call, she practiced even harder. Unfortunately, she began to suffer a series of small, nagging injuries. The harder she practiced, the more she aggravated her injuries. She felt trapped. She told her coaches that she knew she had to train harder to reach the top, but that every time she pushed herself she got injured.

For the first time in her life Cathy began to doubt herself. Her fear of injury caused her to be a little less aggressive during her routines, which in turn caused her performance to decline. Her confidence was at an all-time low. Skating had always been the thing in her life that kept her going and she wasn't skating well. To make matters worse, she felt alone with nobody to turn to. She was separated from her family and because she was so busy training, she had not made many new friends. To avoid disappointing her parents, especially her mother, Cathy had not told them very much about what was going on. Eventually, Cathy became so depressed that she had trouble getting up in the morning. She started to miss training sessions. Her school work declined and she began talking about quitting school and giving up skating. One poor performance followed another, and Cathy eventually dropped out of the skating club and returned home. She described herself as a nobody.

Cathy's story shows some of the dangers of putting all your energy in one area. Instead of trying out new experiences and learning more about herself, Cathy allowed her Olympic dream to dominate her life. Early on, she defined herself as a skater. This gave her an identity. She wasn't worried about finding a career or building relationships because she devoted so much of her time and energy to skating. It's true that you need to devote long hours to practice and conditioning if you want to be a successful athlete, but it's also important to spend enough time learning who you are by exploring different options and experiences. Not only will this exploration help you define who you are, but it may also make you a better athlete by teaching you better ways to manage stress or cope with performance problems. Cathy was an excellent athlete but she didn't know herself very well. She wasn't prepared to handle the poor performances that threatened her dream.

Learning more about yourself helps you begin to define who you are. Sometimes people label themselves before they really know who they are. You may have already labeled yourself as an athlete without taking the time to find out more about your values, needs, and nonsport interests. One way to see how well you know your nonsport identity is to think about how you would describe yourself to a stranger if you couldn't use any information related to your sport involvement.

Do you have trouble knowing where to start or what to talk about? Does the information come from how you feel about yourself or from the way that others would describe you? Do you talk about your skills, values, and interests? If you are able to describe yourself easily, it probably means that you have a good idea of who you are, and you may be well on your way to self-understanding.

If you have trouble describing yourself without using sports, it may mean that you don't know yourself very well or, like Cathy, you're putting all of your energy into your athletic career. To establish your personal identity you must explore values, needs, interests, and skills, and then select those that seem most consistent with your beliefs about yourself. You learn about yourself by trying out new experiences. You learn from both your successes and your failures. Finding out who you are is a process that continues throughout your life. The exercises on self-exploration in chapter 5 will help you gather information so you can begin to define who you are. This information may be important as you make decisions about beginning college or starting your nonsport career.

DECIDING WHETHER COLLEGE IS FOR YOU

As you explore your identity throughout your high school years, you'll face many decisions about what type of person you would like to become in the future. One aspect of your identity will be your future career. As early as your freshman year you'll be asked to decide whether you would like to go on to college after high school or whether you would prefer to pursue a career that doesn't require a college degree. Because very few young people become professional athletes directly from high school, those who aren't college bound often select high school programs that train them for vocational positions such as electrician, auto mechanic, or secretary.

Choosing a program of study for high school may be one of the first major decisions you'll have to face concerning your future career. You'll have to consider your abilities, interests, and your sense of personal identity. You'll also have to decide the number of courses you'll need to take in certain areas and the level of difficulty for each course. These decisions won't be easy for some people. Others may already know what type of program they would like. Your guidance counselors in your junior and senior high schools can help you make this decision, so they are important support people at this point. Your parents can provide additional support as you make this decision.

In making your decision about your high school plan, you may find worksheet 2.1 helpful. Remember that different types of colleges accept people with different abilities, so just because you aren't a straight A student doesn't mean that you can't go to college.

If you answered yes to five or more of the even-numbered items, you may be interested in considering a vocational track in high school. On the

---

Worksheet 2.1:

High School Program Decision Check Sheet

Mark either Yes or No to best show your feelings about each of the following statements.

1. I like most school subjects. *Yes No*

2. I can't wait to get out of school. *Yes No*

3. I'm willing to take courses that don't interest me so that I can complete my degree. *Yes No*

4. I prefer to work with my hands. *Yes No*

5. I enjoy learning new things from books. *Yes No*

6. I can't wait to get out there and work. *Yes No*

7. I like to read about peoples' ideas and thoughts. *Yes No*

8. I like to read about how things work. *Yes No*

9. It's important for me to find out more about life before I hold down a full-time job. *Yes No*

10. I want an income as soon as possible. *Yes No*

11. I'm willing to make some financial sacrifices to go to college. *Yes No*

12. For me, the time and expense of college just don't seem worth it. *Yes No*

other hand, if you answered yes to five or more of the odd-numbered items, you may prefer a college-bound track. If your responses are mixed between both odd- and even-numbered items, you may want to discuss your decision further with your guidance counselor or other support persons.

Vocational Planning for the Non-College-Bound High School Athlete

If you don't want to go on to college you may be considering several options including technical careers, service careers, or positions related to sports that don't require a college degree. You may decide that you would like to pursue a career in which you are able to use technical, hands-on knowledge about products or machinery as, for example, a computer repair specialist or a cable television installer. On the other hand, you may prefer to work with people in a service career as a salesperson, travel agent, or chef. In either case, your high school vocational program may prepare you to work when you graduate, or it may prepare you to be an apprentice while collecting additional specialized training under the supervision of a tradesperson like a carpenter or plumber. Many careers, such as dental hygienist, electrician, or real estate agent, require that you have a certificate or license before you can practice legally. Community colleges, technical career institutes, adult education programs, and businesses may provide additional training and certification opportunities for high school graduates who have chosen not to seek a college degree.

You may want to look at some of the books that provide information about careers that don't require a college degree. For example, the *Occupations Outlook Handbook* and the *Encyclopedia of Careers* are available in your high school guidance office and in your public library. Appendix A lists additional references that might be helpful.

A third area you may be considering if you don't wish to go on to college is a career in professional sport. Planning for a career in sport requires a thorough assessment of your abilities and your potential as a player. Your high school coach or a well-meaning parent isn't qualified to provide such an evaluation. Before you put all of your hopes and dreams into professional sport, be sure to be evaluated repeatedly by professionals in the field. Only a few sports, such as tennis, baseball, and ice hockey, recruit athletes directly out of high school. Other sports may not provide you with enough money to live on. Sports like golf usually require that you spend many years practicing your skills while making only a little money. Players on the minitours must often pay their travel expenses, which may be greater than their winnings. This is particularly true in women's sports, where earnings are often less than in men's sports.

If you're fortunate enough to be able to participate in professional sport directly out of high school, you may need to supplement your income with earnings from other jobs either during the off-season or on a part-time basis. An interesting and worthwhile part-time job may lead to a future career for some athletes.

Criteria for Selecting a College

If you've decided that you would like to go on to college after high school, you'll be making a number of decisions during your high school experience. In the first two years of high school, you'll be working with your high school guidance counselor to select courses that you'll need for entrance into college. You'll select some of these courses by the types of college you wish to attend and your interests and abilities. You'll choose other courses because they are required for participation in intercollegiate athletics. We discuss these requirements later in this chapter. Perhaps the biggest decision you'll be making, however, is which college to attend. This is a difficult decision for most high school seniors, but especially for athletes, who have a number of extra things to consider.

Your first decision may be to decide what role sports will play in making your college choice. You'll need to decide if participating in your sport during college is going to be a primary reason in the selection process or if it will play a less important role in your choice. You may want to ask yourself these questions at this point:

1. How would I feel if I couldn't play my sport in college?
2. Am I ready to let go of my sport right now?
3. Do I really have the ability to play college sport at any level?
4. Would I be willing to sacrifice majoring in a specific field to attend a college that would allow me to play my sport?
5. What would happen if I chose a college and then couldn't participate in my sport there because I was injured or disqualified?
6. Am I willing to make sacrifices in friendships and social life to meet the demands of college sport?
7. Would playing my sport in intramurals be enough to satisfy my need for college sport participation?

If, after answering these questions, you're feeling more committed than ever to becoming a college athlete, then you'll probably be making many of your college decisions based on your ability to play. If, on the other hand, you feel uncertain about some of your responses to these questions, your college decision will probably be more of a compromise. In either case, you may want to discuss your responses to these questions with some of your support team, such as your coach, your guidance counselor, and your parents.

Academic Eligibility for Intercollegiate Athletes

If you want to be able to play and practice during your freshman year at a Division I or II college, you have to meet academic standards set by the National Collegiate Athletic Association (NCAA) (see Table 2.1). The rules that control freshman eligibility differ by NCAA Division I, II, or III and are outlined in the *NCAA Guide for the College-Bound Student-Athlete*. This booklet is available from the NCAA, 6201 College Boulevard, Overland Park, Kansas 66211-2422. Beyond the NCAA regulations, individual colleges or conferences may have freshman eligibility rules that are more demanding than the NCAA's. For example, if you're hoping to attend an Ivy League school, you may need a very high class rank, excellent grades in advanced or honors courses, and outstanding Scholastic Aptitude Test (SAT) or American College Test (ACT) scores. You need to keep these rules in mind as you select your high school courses.

In January 1993, the NCAA Initial Eligibility Clearinghouse was established as a separate organization. The Clearinghouse ensures consistent interpretation of NCAA initial eligibility for prospective student-athletes at all NCAA member institutions. If you're planning to play at Division I or Division II, it's your responsibility to make sure that the Clearinghouse receives all the documents it needs to certify you. These documents are your Student Release Form, official transcripts from every high school you have attended, and a copy of your SAT or ACT results. Information about the NCAA Initial Eligibility Clearinghouse is available from your high school guidance counselor or from the Clearinghouse at P.O. Box 4043, Iowa City, Iowa 52243-4043.

Let's begin by looking at some of the differences in the NCAA divisions and eligibility requirements. What we're presenting is information about general differences between the divisions. You should understand that there can be large differences between colleges in each division. Even within a single college you may find some sports that are Division I and some that are Division III. Also, the NCAA changes academic eligibility requirements on occasion, so you should check the latest eligibility guidelines.

Division I. Division I represents the highest level of intercollegiate competition. Colleges and universities in Division I offer full and partial scholarships in many, but not all, sports. A full scholarship will typically pay for your tuition and fees, room and board, and books. If you don't pass the requirements for freshman eligibility, you can't receive an athletic scholarship but are still eligible for institutional financial aid based on financial need.

As of August 1, 1995, any athlete who wishes to compete in Division I as a freshman must have met the following standards:

1. The student-athlete must have graduated from high school.
2. The student-athlete must have successfully completed a core curriculum of at least 13 academic courses during grades 9 through 12, which must include

   A. three years of English (for example, literature, composition, vocabulary development, analytical reading, oral communication, grammar),

   B. two years of mathematics (for example, algebra, geometry, trigonometry, statistics, calculus),

   C. two years of social science (for example, history, social science, economics, geography, psychology, sociology, government, political science, anthropology),

   D. two years natural or physical science, including at least one full year of laboratory classes if offered by the high school (for example, biology, chemistry, physics, environmental science, earth science, physical science), and

   E. two years of additional academic courses (for example, foreign language, computer science, philosophy, comparative religion).

3. The student-athlete must have achieved a high school grade point average and standardized test score (either the combined math and verbal scores from the SAT or the composite score on the ACT) that would meet the requirements specified in table 2.1.

Division II. Division II represents the second highest level of intercollegiate competition. Division II colleges offer a smaller number of full and partial scholarships than do Division I schools. As of August 1, 1995,

Table 2.1: NCAA Academic Requirements

Core GPA	Minimum required SAT	Minimum required ACT
Above 2.500	700	17
2.500	700	17
2.475	710	18
2.450	720	18
2.425	730	18
2.400	740	18
2.375	750	18
2.350	760	19
2.325	770	19
2.300	780	19
2.275	790	19
2.250	800	19
2.225	810	20
2.200	820	20
2.175	830	20
2.150	840	20
2.125	850	20
2.100	860	21
2.075	870	21
2.050	880	21
2.025	890	21
2.000	900	21
Below 2.000	Not eligible	Not eligible

the NCAA requires that all entering freshman athletes meet the following academic standards to be eligible to play:

1. The student-athlete must have graduated from high school.
2. The student-athlete must have achieved at least a 2.0 grade point average and successfully complete the same core curriculum required of Division I student-athletes.

3. The student-athlete must have achieved a combined SAT score of at least 700 or an ACT composite score of at least 17.

Students planning to attend a Division II college are permitted to use core courses taken at any time before their initial enrollment at the college.

Division III. Division III represents the lowest level of intercollegiate competition. Even so, competition at this level is keen. Division III colleges aren't permitted to award any type of athletic scholarships. All financial aid is awarded on a financial-need basis. There are no NCAA freshman eligibility requirements for entering Division III student-athletes.

Your College Choice

If participating in college athletics is a primary reason for selecting a particular college, then you'll need to consider several points in choosing a college. First, both high school and college coaches must assess your athletic ability to determine your potential to play at the various collegiate levels. Most Division I or II college sports programs recruit athletes who have the skills to play at that level. Because you're being recruited, however, you shouldn't assume that you'll have the same opportunities to play that you had in high school. As one college athlete told us, "I thought that I was going to be a star on the softball team. I didn't realize that almost every player was captain of her high school team, too. I'm not used to sitting on the bench and when I do get in I try so hard that I screw up. I wonder if I will ever get to play here."

If you're being recruited, you may want to ask recruiting coaches some of the following questions to better assess your potential fit with their program.

- What kinds of academic support services are available for student-athletes?
- Will an academic athletic advisor be assigned to work with me?
- What percentage of the athletes in my sport graduate with their class or after five years?
- How do I compare with the other athletes who are presently in the program? Athletically? Academically?
- What will my schedule be like on a typical day in season?
- What will my schedule be like on a typical day out of season?
- Will I have an opportunity for playing time as a freshman?
- How many other athletes who play my position are being recruited?

If you aren't being recruited, you need to find out if your expectations are realistic. You can ask your coach to contact some college coaches for you. You can develop a personal highlight videotape and an outline of your personal athletic accomplishments and send them directly to coaches at colleges you would like to attend. Your goal should be to get a realistic assessment of your skills. You may not be able to play at a Division I school, but you might have the ability to play at Division III.

You may find out that you aren't being recruited because you lack size, experience, or the proper academic background. You can correct some of these problems by attending a prep school for a year or two. This may give you the opportunity to mature physically and further improve your academic and athletic skills.

Second, you need to match your academic ability to the difficulty level of the academic program you want to pursue. Some college programs are so demanding that you might not have enough time to play a sport and keep up with your studies. Even if you're able to play a sport at a particular college, you may not be able to maintain the grade point average necessary to remain eligible.

Third, you'll want to decide if you like the coaches, the players, the style of play, and the facilities for your sport at that particular school. If you're presently in the process of making a college decision based on athletic participation, you may want to complete worksheet 2.2, the Athlete's College Choice Handicapping Sheet.

Worksheet 2.2:
Athlete's College Choice Handicapping Sheet

Make copies of this sheet and fill it out for each college you're considering. Please rate each college and compare the results.

Name of college or university _____

Opportunity to play my sport
                    Unlikely 1 2 3 4 5 6 7 8 9 10 **Definitely**

Chance that I'll be a starter
                    Unlikely 1 2 3 4 5 6 7 8 9 10 **Definitely**

Chance that I'll be a star player

        Unlikely 1 2 3 4 5 6 7 8 9 10 **Definitely**

Chance that I'll get decent grades

        Unlikely 1 2 3 4 5 6 7 8 9 10 **Definitely**

Chance that I'll like the coach

        Unlikely 1 2 3 4 5 6 7 8 9 10 **Definitely**

Chance that I'll like the team

        Unlikely 1 2 3 4 5 6 7 8 9 10 **Definitely**

Chance that I'll like the facilities

        Unlikely 1 2 3 4 5 6 7 8 9 10 **Definitely**

Opportunity for parents to watch

        Unlikely 1 2 3 4 5 6 7 8 9 10 **Definitely**

Possibility that the team will win

        Unlikely 1 2 3 4 5 6 7 8 9 10 **Definitely**

Add your specific additional considerations below.

_____

        Unlikely 1 2 3 4 5 6 7 8 9 10 **Definitely**

_____

        Unlikely 1 2 3 4 5 6 7 8 9 10 **Definitely**

_____

        Unlikely 1 2 3 4 5 6 7 8 9 10 **Definitely**

_____

        Unlikely 1 2 3 4 5 6 7 8 9 10 **Definitely**

_____

        Unlikely 1 2 3 4 5 6 7 8 9 10 **Definitely**

Total points for this college or university _____

Total points for the most important considerations _____

You should evaluate your responses to the Athlete's College Choice Handicapping Sheet in two ways. First, you should add the numbers that you circled for each item and compare the total points for each college. Second, you should check off the most important questions that you're considering and total only those responses. For example, if opportunity to play, chance to be a starter, chance that you'll like the coach, and opportunity for parents to watch games are your most important concerns, then total your response for these items only.

You can also make additions or deletions to the handicapping list to meet your specific needs. For example, if playing in a particular conference or having a chance to play more than one sport is a consideration, add these items to the handicapping guide. If, for example, athletic facilities aren't important to you, cross it off the list.

Your overall scores on the handicapping exercise give you some important information about the athletic considerations in your college decision. Your next step is to examine nonsport concerns.

For many high school athletes, selecting the right college doesn't depend only on athletic considerations. One athlete, who later went on to earn all-American honors in swimming, transferred from a large university to a smaller Division I school because he felt uncomfortable in the large-school environment. When he was thinking of transferring, he told his advisor, "I came from a small high school and sometimes I feel lost in these big classes with 300 students. The professor comes and lectures for 50 minutes and then leaves. I had no idea how I was doing until I got my first test back after midterms. I'm used to a lot more attention." Another athlete, who plays football at a Division II college, talked about the importance of college location. He said, "I sure miss my friends back home. My teammates are great, but a lot of them are different than me. I came from a small town and all these guys are from the city. It has taken me longer to adjust than I thought it would."

For these students, other qualities of a college became important in selecting the right school. College size, location, academic programs, distance from home, quality of education, and general environment may be the most important considerations for you. Students who consider athletics first in making their college choice will have to weigh these items as well.

Worksheet 2.3, the College Choice Scorecard, will help you to see how important different aspects of college life are to you in making a college choice, whether you are focused on athletics or not.

Besides your gut feelings about what is important in making a college choice, you can use the advice of others. Current students, alumni or

Worksheet 2.3:

College Choice Scorecard

Rank the following college qualities according to their importance to you in making your college choice. Please number the most important quality with a 1 and the least important with a 12.

		College A		College B	
Qualities	*Rank*	*Score*	*Total*	*Score*	*Total*
College size	____	____	____	____	____
Academic programs	____	____	____	____	____
Athletic programs	____	____	____	____	____
Setting	____	____	____	____	____
Appearance	____	____	____	____	____
People at the college	____	____	____	____	____
Facilities and buildings	____	____	____	____	____
Prestige of the college	____	____	____	____	____
Residence halls	____	____	____	____	____
Food	____	____	____	____	____
Social life	____	____	____	____	____
Distance from home	____	____	____	____	____
		Total ____		*Total* ____	

If you have some colleges in mind right now, rate each college in the columns provided with the following scoring: 1 = excellent, 2 = good, 3 = average, 4 = poor, and 5 = horrible. To compare each college for how they meet your most important criteria, add your "rank" plus your score for each item and place that number in the total column for each quality. To get an overall score add up all the scores in the total column for each college. Remember the lower the score the better the match.

alumnae, faculty, and support staff at colleges can be helpful sources of information.

Delayed College Decision

Some athletes may need to delay their college plans until after a major athletic competition. Olympic athletes, for example, may need to wait until after the Olympic Games to start their college careers. Other athletes may attend college part-time at a convenient site while they are competing and then transfer to a college that is more suitable to them after their competition is over. In this case, the college decision is often one of convenience, so finding a college that adapts to their particular schedule may be most important.

Although it may seem like a simple decision to delay your college education until after you have competed in your sport, you need to consider that most athletes who choose this option never return to school. The Canadian Broadcasting Company's "5th Estate" television program highlighted the dilemma facing many junior hockey players in Canada. If you are drafted by one of the junior hockey programs, you must decide to go with your dream of playing in the National Hockey League (NHL) by playing junior hockey or hope to get a scholarship at a college in the United States. The program showed how many of the athletes never finish high school because of their demanding practice, travel, and competition schedules. Yet only a handful of the junior hockey players ever make it to the NHL.

If you're considering delaying your college decision until your athletic career is over, you should plan to take at least a few courses at a local four-year or community college during your off-season. The prospect of spending four years after you retire from your sport to pursue a college degree may seem like too much of a hurdle to overcome. Taking courses while you're still competing will keep you connected to the educational system and is probably the best way to ensure that you'll eventually achieve your goal of a college education.

Resources Needed in the College Selection Process

The college selection process can be difficult. This is a great time to call together your support team to help you make the best choice possible. Your coaches, prospective coaches, guidance counselors, teachers, college admissions counselors, and your parents can all be wonderful resources at this time. You'll also need to do a great deal of research on your own. Remember, this is *your* future. You need to take an active role in this important decision.

The resources at the back of this book may be especially helpful to you now. Appendix A contains a listing of guides that will help you find information about various colleges across the country. A list of college majors, which may be helpful to you at this point, is located in the next chapter.

In addition, most high school guidance departments have computer programs that will help you identify colleges that fit your specific requirements. For example, if you want to identify colleges in New England that offer programs in business administration and have Division III lacrosse teams, you could get a list of them by answering a few questions on the computer screen. Check with your guidance office for more information about this resource.

Developing Your High School Plan

Now that you've looked over the NCAA rules and the other choices you'll have to consider in preparing for college, you may want to develop a high school academic plan for yourself. Worksheet 2.4 will help you to do this. Of course, you should speak with your guidance counselor and check for any changes in NCAA regulations as you plan for future courses.

Worksheet 2.4:
Your High School Academic Plan

To be eligible to play an intercollegiate sport as a freshman at a Division I or II college, you must successfully complete a core curriculum during high school. You must attain a grade point average of at least a 2.0 and you cannot fail any of your core courses. Use the following chart to plan your course of study. A unit equals a full year of instruction.

English (minimum of three units required)

Course title	Date completed	Grade	Units earned
1. _____	_____	___	_____
2. _____	_____	___	_____
3. _____	_____	___	_____
4. _____	_____	___	_____

Mathematics (minimum of two units required)

Course title	Date completed	Grade	Units earned
1. _____	_____	____	_____
2. _____	_____	____	_____
3. _____	_____	____	_____

Social science (minimum of two units required)

Course title	Date completed	Grade	Units earned
1. _____	_____	____	_____
2. _____	_____	____	_____
3. _____	_____	____	_____

Natural or physical science (minimum of two units required)

Course title	Date completed	Grade	Units earned
1. _____	_____	____	_____
2. _____	_____	____	_____
3. _____	_____	____	_____

Additional academic courses (minimum of two units required)

Course title	Date completed	Grade	Units earned
1. _____	_____	____	_____
2. _____	_____	____	_____

CHAPTER SUMMARY

The high school years are filled with many decisions for student-athletes. Some decisions are made on hopes and dreams for athletics, while others are based on other career aspirations.

From this chapter, you should have learned the following:

1. High school is a time to learn about your personal identity.

2. Part of your personal identity has to do with your initial plans for your future career.

3. The biggest decision you'll make early in high school is whether or not you'll go to college.

4. You'll probably take your athletic abilities and desires into account when you decide on your high school plan of studies, your college choice, or your vocational goals.

5. College choice requires thinking about many factors, including athletic participation, your academic abilities, academic programs, and the college environment.

6. NCAA rules may affect your ability to play at certain levels of intercollegiate competition.

7. Whether you plan to attend college or not, you should develop a program of studies in high school that will help you with future goals and opportunities.

Chapter 3

College

Those who play intercollegiate sports will find the college years filled with important challenges. You'll continue to learn more about yourself and further develop your personal identity. If you are away from home, family, and friends, you may find that you need to rely more on yourself. You'll meet and interact with people from backgrounds much different from yours. You'll need to learn how to balance the increased demands of your sport and your academics. You'll be further refining your career goals and making academic choices to meet these goals. You'll be preparing yourself for life after college and making major decisions about your career, sports, and relationships. Your four or five years of college will surely be challenging.

In this chapter, we'll provide you with information to help you prepare for some of these challenges. In particular, we'll address five important tasks that face college student-athletes:

1. Adjusting to college
2. Developing a personal and career identity
3. Selecting a major
4. Balancing sports, academics, and social relationships
5. Preparing for life after college

You'll need to rely on your skills, plus identify and use the new support people who will become part of your college world. We'll help you anticipate what might happen and help you develop a game plan for a successful college career. Let's begin by looking at some of the adjustments that you may have to make as you enter college.

ADJUSTING TO COLLEGE

If you're like most student-athletes, you'll find that college is much different from high school. You'll probably need to make many physical, psychological, academic, and social adjustments. To help you anticipate some of the adjustments that you may have to make, we'll review what other athletes have told us about their experience in adjusting to college.

To begin with, college practices are physically tough. In high school you may have been the biggest, fastest, and strongest player, but now you'll be surrounded by players who were the biggest, fastest, and strongest players for their schools. You'll probably find that you'll be practicing longer and harder than you did in high school. The coaches will demand more of you and push you to your limits. This will help your sport skills, but you'll find that you're more tired and have less time and energy. With informal workouts and weight training in the off-season, you'll be involved in your sport year-round. The time and energy drains on you will be great. As one gymnast put it, "I couldn't believe how tired I felt once practices started my freshman year. I would nap during the day before practice and still find myself falling asleep as I'd try to study at night. It sure is a lot different than high school."

In addition, you were probably comfortable as the star in high school. You played most of the game. You got a lot of recognition. You were the go-to person when your team needed a big play. Now you're just one of several promising recruits. As a freshman, you'll have to learn to blend into the team. Whether you play an individual sport or a team sport, you must pay your dues. You'll have to earn the respect of the coaching staff and learn how to be accepted by your teammates. You may have to learn to be a role player or adjust to sitting the bench. You'll need to make these psychological adjustments and more.

Adjusting to the academic demands of college can be just as difficult. You'll have all the academic demands of your nonathlete classmates, but you may not be as well prepared academically or have as much time or energy for study. A basketball player described her adjustment this way:

"The thing that I remember most about my freshman year was the change that took place for me during midterms. My first few weeks of school I went to my classes, did a little bit of studying, and played in the pickup games with the team in the afternoon. Before I knew it, October 15 rolled in and practices started at the same time that midterm exams and the first sets of papers became due. I went from having plenty of time to playing catch-up the rest of the semester."

Many colleges recruit and admit athletes who don't have the same high school grades and SAT or ACT scores as their regular students. You may have had grades and test scores adequate for admission but be in classes with students who got higher grades in high school and who scored higher on their SAT or ACT tests.

In addition, most colleges won't allow students to work more than 20 hours a week in on-campus jobs. College officials feel that anything more would seriously affect a student's academic performance. However, as a college athlete, you may find that between practices, games, travel, game film review sessions, and informal activities related to sport, you're putting in well beyond 20 hours per week. Clearly, you'll have many academic challenges to overcome.

If you're away from home for the first time, this can be a difficult period for you socially. You may have been very popular in high school because of the visibility you got as an athlete, but in college you might know only the people you were introduced to during your campus visit. You may have to adjust to teammates, roommates, and classmates who come from different racial, cultural, and socioeconomic backgrounds.

Some faculty and students may appreciate you and your athletic abilities, while others may resent you for receiving a scholarship because you're an athlete. College athletes are heroes to many people in the college community; others believe that athletes are spoiled, overprivileged, and academically inferior.

Because your best friends, family, and other support people may not be close enough for you to see on a regular basis, you need to develop new support people. Your teammates may not be able to provide you with all the different types of support that you need. One football player described his experience this way: "I got to college in August before school started, so I could play preseason. I hooked up with a couple of other football players that first day and we became roommates. We pretty much did everything together, you know, typical jock stuff. The only problem was I couldn't talk to them about how I felt playing only on the dummy squad while all of them were getting to play some varsity." This football player's roommates may have eased his social transition into college, but they weren't able to assist him with his feelings about not playing.

Recognize that the physical, psychological, academic, and social adjustments that you face are interrelated. For example, if you're tired and not playing well, it could affect your ability to concentrate on your studies or your interest in going out to meet new people. Planning for your adjustment to college and adding new members to your support team will ensure that your academic and athletic experiences will be enjoyable.

Although you face many challenges as a college student-athlete, your transition doesn't have to overflow with problems. Most athletes make a relatively smooth transition into collegiate life. To help you do the same, let's examine the case of one athlete, Mary, who was forced to make several minor adjustments on her way to a successful first year in college. As you read through the case, identify the concerns that Mary was forced to deal with, along with any personal skills or special support people who assisted her during her transition. After you finish reading the case, compare your list of issues to those outlined in highlight box 3.1. We'll use Mary's story throughout the chapter as we further examine the tasks you'll face as a college student-athlete.

Mary's Story

Mary, an outstanding basketball player in high school, decided to accept a scholarship from a large university in the Northeast. She arrived at school with the other freshmen and waited in a long line of students to find her room assignment. When Mary finally got to the registration table, she was relieved to get a note from the assistant basketball coach along with her dorm assignment. The note welcomed her to campus and told her to report to the athletic office later that day to get help with class registration and scheduling. Mary found her room and met her roommate, who was also on basketball scholarship.

Later that day Mary and her roommate reported to the athletic office and met with one of the assistant coaches, who doubled up as an academic advisor. Although Mary had not settled on a major, she had checked off physical education as her intended major on her application. She thought that she might want to coach and believed that most high school coaches taught PE. Mary was pleased when her advisor handed her a course schedule that showed only five courses. The advisor told her that if she felt that five courses would be too much, she could drop one anytime during the first four weeks of classes without any problems. If she did drop a class, however, she would have to make up the credits in summer school, take an overload in a future semester, or return to school for a fifth year of study. All of Mary's classes met in the mornings, so she could have her afternoons free.

When classes began a few days later Mary quickly got into a routine. She would attend classes in the mornings, study a little in the early afternoon, play in the pickup games from 4:00 to 6:00, take a shower, and have dinner. At night Mary went to a study hall that all freshman athletes were required to attend for two hours each school night except Friday. Mary didn't mind the study halls because it gave her a chance to meet the other freshman athletes.

Mary quickly became friends with two of the women on the softball team who came from the town next to where she had grown up. They lived on the same floor and Mary felt comfortable with them because they enjoyed sports and liked many of the things that she did. The other women on the floor were more into clothes and their social lives. They seemed to have a lot of money and spent a lot of time partying. Mary spent most of her free time in her old sweats with her softball buddies and was too busy to do much partying.

Mary knew that college was going to be different from high school and that she might not be as popular, but she hoped that once basketball season started she would become better known. Mary soon discovered, however, that some students and faculty disliked athletes and stereotyped all of them as dumb, spoiled jocks. She overheard some of the women on her floor complaining that athletes got all the privileges and didn't even have to pay for their education. It bothered Mary that some students could dislike her just because she was an athlete.

Mary had managed to keep up with her studies but noticed a big change when official practice began. She had most of her midterm exams during mid-October and used every available minute to study and do research for her term papers. Her academic advisor had done a good job of helping Mary budget her time and plan for her exams. The hard work paid off as Mary was able to pull three Cs and two Bs on her exams and turn in the first draft of her English term paper on time.

The big adjustment came in basketball. Mary thought she was in great shape, but after practice every muscle in her body ached. She

> *was now at the gym by 3:30 for taping and rarely left before 6:45. She had barely enough time to eat before reporting to her 7:00 to 9:00 study hall. Mary was very tired at first, but kept giving it everything she had.*
>
> *Although she felt she was playing well, Mary was getting limited playing time in the scrimmages. The coaches yelled at her constantly. She noticed that a few of the veteran players seemed rather cold to her. Mary wasn't sure if the players' reactions to her were just part of paying her dues or if they didn't like her. It was true that Mary was the only player on the team who hadn't grown up in a large city, but she had always felt welcome in the preseason pickup games. As the days went by Mary came to realize that most of her teammates sat together in the cafeteria. Mary had to learn to go over to them and start conversations. She worked hard to be accepted.*
>
> *Mary started the season on the bench and was getting 8 to 10 minutes of playing time per game. Even though she had not expected to start, it still hurt. Mary got her big break in December, when the starting center went down with an injury. She stepped into the starting role and played well, finishing the season as the second-leading scorer and tied for top rebounder. What was more important was that she felt accepted and valued by her teammates*

By overcoming the concerns listed in highlight box 3.1, Mary was able to make the adjustment to college life and thereby accomplish the first of the five major tasks that you'll face as a college student-athlete. Before we discuss those, we'll introduce you to some of the support services available to you in college. Next we'll help you develop your plan for adjusting to college.

Let's begin by looking at some of the support services that will be available to you in college.

Academic-Athletic Advising

Most Division I colleges, and a growing number of Division II and III colleges, have special academic advisors who coordinate a variety of support services to help you grow as a student and an athlete. In some of the larger universities, the academic advising staff provide athletes with special orientation programs, tutoring, study skills programs, career counseling, personal counseling, academic advisement, and life skill development. At the very least, academic athletic advisors provide academic advisement and arrange for tutors, study halls, and academic

Highlight Box 3.1

Mary's Concerns
While Adjusting to College

Physical

1. Mary had to adjust to the physical demands of college practices.
2. Mary was often fatigued and had to make sure she got plenty of rest.

Psychological

1. Mary had to adjust to sitting the bench during the beginning of the season.
2. The coaches yelled at her and pushed her to be a tougher player.
3. Mary had to cope with some antijock bias.

Academic

1. Mary had to plan her academic schedule.
2. Mary had to select an academic major.
3. Mary had to keep up with her studies.

Social

1. Mary had to learn to make new friends.
2. Mary had to adjust to being with people from different socioeconomic, ethnic, and cultural backgrounds.
3. Mary needed to find a way to be accepted by her teammates.

Other

1. Mary had to learn how to balance her academic, athletic, and social time commitments.

support like writing skills development and time management. Student-athletes should investigate the academic support services for athletes at colleges that they are considering.

Academic Support Services

Most colleges have academic support services for the general student population. These usually include an orientation program, writing centers, resources for students with learning disabilities, tutoring services, and general academic advisement. These are wonderful resources for student-athletes, but you need to find out about them and actively seek assistance.

Student Services

Almost every college has a group of professionals who provide specialized support services to students under the general heading of student services or office of student affairs. Included within this area are housing, student activities, career planning and placement, financial aid, counseling center, and dean of students. These services are available to you as part of the general student population.

Sports Medicine Services

Many colleges have comprehensive sports medicine services. These professional physicians, physical therapists, athletic trainers, counselors, and sport psychologists can help you prevent or cope with injuries and improve your athletic performance. Such professionals are good resources because they have a sense of what it's like to be an athlete, and they understand the special needs that you have as a student-athlete.

Other Sources of Support

Beyond the general support services described above, you'll find many faculty, administrators, and staff who can be valuable sources of support. In addition, you'll have an opportunity to join student organizations and clubs that can be excellent sources of support and introduce you to a variety of students.

We've listed some of the activities that you can take advantage of on your college campus in worksheet 3.1. Try to do at least four of these activities each year.

Now it's time for you to develop your game plan for adjusting to college. To begin with, you may want to talk with your coach, friends who are already in college, and your parents to get more information about what college will really be like. As you learned in the chapter on transitions, experience with one transition can help prepare you for future transitions. As you think about the tasks that you may face in college, remember to

Worksheet 3.1:

Career Support Activities

Please list the date that you participated in any of the following career support activities in the space provided. Each activity can be done more than once.

Activity	*Date completed*
1. Attend first-year student orientation program	_____
2. Tour career services office	_____
3. Attend group career information session	_____
4. Use computer-assisted career counseling	_____
5. Attend individual career counseling session	_____
6. Attend workshop on job-hunting strategies	_____
7. Attend graduate school fair	_____
8. View video library of career fields	_____
9. Attend jobs fair	_____
10. Review career library resource materials	_____
11. Participate in career mentoring program	_____
12. Listen to guest speakers about careers	_____
13. Meet with academic advisor	_____
14. Meet with athletic academic advisor	_____
15. Complete career internship	_____
16. Take career development course	_____
17. Attend resume and cover letter workshop	_____
18. Register with career services placement	_____
19. Interview faculty member about careers	_____
20. Speak with alumni about careers	_____

identify your coping resources and any additional physical and mental skills that may help you adjust to college. As shown in highlight box 3.1, Mary faced many issues in adjusting to college. We want you to begin planning your transition into college by completing worksheet 3.2.

When you've completed Your Game Plan for Entering College, you may find it useful to share your work with members of your support team. By

Worksheet 3.2:

Your Game Plan for Entering College

A. List any concerns that you have about adjusting to college.

Physical

1. _____
2. _____
3. _____
4. _____
5. _____

Psychological

1. _____
2. _____
3. _____
4. _____
5. _____

Academic

1. _____
2. _____
3. _____
4. _____
5. _____

Social

1. _____
2. _____
3. _____
4. _____
5. _____

Other

1. _____
2. _____
3. _____
4. _____
5. _____

B. Use circles, squares, or stars to highlight any concerns that might be interrelated.

C. For each area of concern list any positive coping skills that you used in the past that may help you with this situation.

Area of concern _____

Skills to be used _____

_____

_____

D. For each area of concern list any support people who may be able to assist you and what kind of support they may provide. Remember that you may have several support people for each area of concern.

Area of concern _____

Name of support persons   *Type of support*

1. _____   1. _____

2. _____   2. _____

3. _____   3. _____

4. _____   4. _____

5. _____   5. _____

6. _____   6. _____

having others evaluate your plan, you can ensure that you'll use the best skills and resources available to you.

PERSONAL AND CAREER IDENTITY

In chapter 2, we introduced you to the second main task of college life, establishing your personal identity. During the college years you begin to solidify your identity by choosing a career and other interests, such as politics, religion, or social causes. Remember that to make good decisions you need to have the right information. This holds true when you're making decisions about your identity.

The identity development process has two parts. The first part is called *exploratory behavior.* Exploratory behavior is another way of saying that you have to get the right information to make good choices. Your experiences in college can give you many opportunities to learn about different career options, interests, values, cultures, religions, types of people, political views, and a host of other important issues. It's up to you, however, to seek out these opportunities. This may seem like an easy thing to do, but you may have to push yourself to explore options. For example, recall that Mary was introduced to some new experiences when she had to deal with antijock bias and learn to get along in an environment filled with socioeconomic and cultural differences. She was so busy with her sport and academics, however, that she had not actively checked out possible career options or spent much time with people not involved in sports.

After you've explored options by meeting new people and trying out different behaviors, you'll be in a better position to complete the second part of the identity development process, which is *commitment.* Commitment occurs when you select an option and by doing so reject others. For example, if you choose to be a psychology major, you're making a commitment to that field and rejecting other majors. This doesn't mean that you're locked into this major forever, but you've chosen to put your energies into this area, which now becomes part of your identity.

You should realize the risk of making commitments before engaging in exploratory behavior. It's easy to select a major just because you did well in that subject in high school or your roommate is taking the same courses. You could luck out, but your chances for success and happiness are much greater if you take the time to explore your values, needs, interests, and skills before you commit to an area of study. In fact, there is evidence that if you select a major compatible with your interests, you'll achieve better grades.

As a student-athlete you'll be subject to many time and energy drains that interfere with opportunities for exploratory behavior. We'll give you some resources to help you manage your time more efficiently in the section "Balancing Sports, Academics, and Social Relationships."

We've designed the chapters on self-exploration and career exploration to help you begin your exploratory behavior. The more you know about yourself and the career options available to you, the more likely it is that you'll make commitments to options that will help you achieve your academic, athletic, and personal goals. One of the first decisions that you'll face is selecting a major.

SELECTING A MAJOR

You may feel a lot of pressure to select a major or career track. You may have heard the question "What are you going to do when you graduate from school" a hundred times already. It may be tempting to commit to something quickly to relieve the pressure. But in doing so you run the danger of making a bad choice. You can improve your chances of selecting the right major and successfully developing your personal identity if you engage in exploratory behavior before you make any commitments.

Many colleges will allow you to complete your first year or two as an undeclared major. By selecting this status, you give yourself an opportunity to explore options while taking a general course of study. As with any decision, the better the information, the better the chance of a good decision. Yet many student-athletes select college majors without examining their values, needs, interests, and skills, or without exploring various career options. Selecting a major is a serious undertaking that has major implications for academic success and future careers. Unfortunately, many students make quick decisions. Consider the experience of these student-athletes.

"When I got to college I knew a lot about the softball program, but not much about anything else. When they asked me what I wanted to major in, I said English because I did well in it in high school. I never really gave much thought to what I wanted to do for a career."

"I kind of went along with the flow. I got to school and registered for the same classes as my roommate. I figured we could study together and that would be a great help to both of us. Some of my teammates were in the same classes, so I never thought much about the future. Now I'm a senior in teacher education and I'm not sure if that is what I want to do, but it's too late to change that now."

In each case, the athlete did *not* engage in exploratory behavior. It's easy to get so wrapped up in your sport, academics, and social life that you don't take the time to explore the many opportunities that college can provide. You'll find that if you take the time to see what options are available, you'll probably make better decisions about what to major in or pursue as a career.

We described how Mary initially fell into the trap of making a quick decision about her major. She chose physical education because she wanted to coach, but she knew little about physical education as a profession. As it turned out Mary became frustrated with all the science courses she was required to take in her sophomore year. She was not very interested in the subject matter, which made studying even more of a task. Eventually she went to the career development office, where she completed a battery of tests and worked with a counselor. From this information, Mary realized that her true interests were in art and helping people. She transferred into the art therapy program with a minor in psychology.

As you have learned, many colleges will allow you to choose an undeclared major for your first year or two in school. This is particularly helpful if you aren't sure what you would like to do or haven't taken the time to explore possible options. Whatever the case, you'll typically be required to select a major by your junior year. You must choose wisely because to remain eligible you must meet an NCAA progress rule. This means that you have to be making progress toward a degree by taking the courses that are necessary for that major. The NCAA established the rule to prevent athletes from taking easy courses only to remain eligible. Your academic athletic advisor is responsible for reporting whether you're making satisfactory progress toward completing your degree.

Before selecting a major, it's important to know your interests, values, needs, and skills, and what college majors would be consistent with those personal characteristics. Recall that Mary wanted to be a coach but thought that the only way to become one was to teach physical education. She didn't realize what physical education teachers really do nor did she know what background coaches typically have. Clearly, Mary needed to do some exploratory behavior before she made this important choice.

Few of us recognize how many options we really have. For example, as an athlete you should have a good sense of careers related to sports. Let's test your knowledge by using worksheet 3.3.

If you found that you have limited knowledge of careers related to sport, you're not alone. Even though you've been part of the sport world for many years, it wouldn't be unusual if you didn't realize how many options you had available to you in this one field. We've designed the chapter on career exploration to help you learn about more career options. Remember that the more you explore and the more you know about different careers, the better the information you'll have to select a college major.

A good way to start your exploration of possible majors is to learn more about the sport-related careers that you identified in worksheet 3.3. For

Worksheet 3.3:
Your Possible Athletic Careers

A. Please list as many careers related to sport as you can think of in the spaces below.

_____

_____

_____

_____

_____

_____

_____

_____

_____

_____

B. Now compare your list to our list of some of the careers related to sport described in appendix B.

C. List any of the careers related to sport that you want to know more about in the space below.

_____

_____

_____

example, if you wanted to learn more about sport psychology or athletic equipment design, you could start by talking with your guidance counselors or looking through books such as the *Occupational Outlook Handbook* or the *Dictionary of Occupational Titles.* Through these resources you could learn what people in these careers do and what academic major and additional training such careers require.

Before we go any further, it may be helpful for you to examine some of the college majors available to you. Unlike high school, where you had few options, college offers a wide variety of areas of study. You'll be able to select a major and minor area of study, which will each require that you take specific courses. You'll be free to choose other courses, called electives. Worksheet 3.4 will help you discover some of your options.

Worksheet 3.4:
College Majors Finder for Athletes

Use the following scale to rate your interest in each of the majors listed below:

3 = Very interested
2 = Somewhat interested
1 = Slightly interested
0 = Not interested at all
U = I don't know enough about this major,
but want to learn more about it

_____ Agriculture	_____ Engineering
_____ Animal science	_____ Foreign languages
_____ Food science	_____ Medical technology
_____ Conservation	_____ Dental hygiene
_____ Natural resources	_____ Radiology
_____ Architecture	_____ Art therapy
_____ Environmental design	_____ Occupational therapy
_____ American studies	_____ Physical therapy
_____ International studies	_____ Respiratory therapy
_____ Business management	_____ Speech pathology/audiology
_____ Banking and finance	_____ Health care administration
_____ Marketing	_____ Sports medicine
_____ Communication	_____ Athletic training
_____ Journalism	_____ Nursing
_____ Advertising	_____ Premedicine
_____ Broadcasting	_____ Predentistry
_____ Public relations	_____ Preveterinary
_____ Computer science	_____ Prepharmacy
_____ Education	_____ Home economics
_____ Special education	_____ Food sciences
_____ Health education	_____ Nutrition
_____ Physical education	_____ Textiles and clothing

_____ Fashion design

_____ Prelaw

_____ Legal assisting

_____ English

_____ Comparative literature

_____ Biology

_____ Botany

_____ Ecology

_____ Mathematics

_____ Military science

_____ Women's studies

_____ Parks and recreation management

_____ Philosophy

_____ Religion

_____ Astronomy

_____ Chemistry

_____ Geology

_____ Physics

_____ Psychology

_____ Criminal justice

_____ Law enforcement

_____ Public administration

_____ Social work

_____ Sociology

_____ Anthropology

_____ Archeology

_____ Economics

_____ Geography

_____ History

_____ Urban studies

_____ Visual and performing arts

_____ Graphic design

_____ Dramatic arts

_____ Dance

_____ Fine arts

_____ Music

Our goal in having you complete the College Majors Finder isn't to have you select a major now, but to help you identify majors that you want to learn more about. If you list all the majors that you rated as 3 (very interesting), and those that you marked as U (I want to learn more about it), you'll have a number of options to discuss with your guidance counselor or to look up in the resource guides listed in appendix A.

By exploring college majors and careers related to sport, you've begun to learn how to do the career exploration necessary to make good career decisions. In chapter 6, we'll provide you with additional tools to gather career information that will help you select a college major that will prepare you for a particular career field.

BALANCING SPORTS, ACADEMICS, AND SOCIAL RELATIONSHIPS

Although the fourth task of college life—balancing sports, academics, and social relationships—may not seem to relate directly to career and life planning, it's an important life skill that will help you succeed not only in college but also throughout your work life. As you learn about some of the difficulties you might come across in trying to adjust to college, you may have questions about how you would balance your athletic involvement with your course work and your personal life. Will there be enough time to study after practices and games? Will college be all work and no play? Will I be able to handle all of my schoolwork without my parents around to check on me?

On the other hand, you may not worry at all right now, but later find yourself in over your head with last-minute work. Or, you may find yourself in control of your sport schedule and all of your schoolwork, but fail to work at your social life and feel like you don't have a friend in the world.

Learning how to manage your time effectively will be one of the most important skills you can master in adjusting to college and your future career. It's not just a matter of getting your work done. It's also a matter of enjoying your life at college and developing friendships and relationships that will last for the rest of your life. Time for yourself, for relaxation, for friends, and for just plain fun will be important parts of your college life. You've probably heard adults say over and over that "these are the best years of your life." When you're a college athlete, knowing how to manage your time will probably determine whether this becomes true for you.

Fortunately, you can learn techniques and skills to manage time more effectively, enabling you to balance the many tasks and roles you'll have in college and throughout life. We like to think of these techniques as the five Ps: patterning, prioritizing, planning, preparing, and personalizing. We've developed some exercises to help you learn and use these techniques.

The first technique is *patterning,* which involves looking at the time you spend on required tasks. This will help you determine how much flexible time you have during the week. By seeing the pattern or structure of an actual week, you can plan your time better. The exercise on Worksheet 3.5 will help you look at your weekly time pattern.

Because college students often spend less time in the classroom than they did in high school, they may think at first that they have more free time. College courses, however, require more study time outside class, while other activities may be more time-consuming as well.

In trying to determine how much time you actually have, you may want to fill in worksheet 3.5, which covers the tasks and activities in the week of a typical college athlete.

Worksheet 3.5:

College Activities

Scheduled weekly events (musts): *Examples:* Class hours, practices, mandatory meetings, fitness training, church, part-time work

Activity	*Hours per week*

Personal and frequently repeated activities (flexible times, but necessary to do): *Examples:* Personal health care, sleep, meals, homework, housekeeping chores

Activity	*Hours per week*

Time eaters (frequent but not required activities): *Examples:* Shopping, visiting, talking on the phone, reading, watching TV, attending social or sports events

Activity	*Hours per week*

Occasional events (may take up chunks of time every once in a while):
Examples: Volunteer work, GRE tests, tournaments, special competitions

Activity	*Hours per week*
_____	_____
_____	_____
_____	_____
_____	_____
_____	_____
Total hours per week in all activities	_____

Remember that a week contains only 168 hours. If your total hours exceeded 168, then you need to make some adjustments. What are you going to give up? To answer that question, you'll need to learn how to set priorities and do a better job of planning.

Prioritizing simply means determining which tasks in your life right now are most important to you or are required or necessary. After you place these activities on a weekly or daily schedule, you can add other activities of lesser importance to your time management plan. On worksheet 3.6, you can begin your time management plan by developing a weekly plan of required and important activities.

Now that you've seen how to set priorities and plan, you need to learn a fourth technique, *preparing.* While all college students need to plan for busy times during a semester, college athletes have peak times in their sports as well. These busy times may overlap with midterm or final exams, making the whole time management process twice as difficult. You'll also want to note active times in your personal and social life. The Time Pressures Grid, worksheet 3.7, helps you look at your peak pressure times during the year so that you can manage your time better during these periods.

For academic planning, review the syllabus for each of your courses. Note when projects or major papers are due. Record exam dates, midterm periods, and final exam periods. For your personal and social calendar, be sure to list any special family occasions or holiday family get-togethers.

Worksheet 3.6:
Time Management for Athletes

A weekly planner

This week's top priorities:

1. _____

2. _____

3. _____

*Other activities
(in order of priority):*

1. _____

2. _____

3. _____

Monday A.M.

_____
_____
_____
_____
_____

Monday P.M.

_____
_____
_____
_____
_____

Tuesday A.M.

_____
_____
_____
_____
_____

Tuesday P.M.

_____
_____
_____
_____
_____

Wednesday A.M.

_____
_____
_____
_____
_____

Wednesday P.M.

_____
_____
_____
_____
_____

Thursday A.M.

_____

_____

_____

_____

_____

Thursday P.M.

_____

_____

_____

_____

Friday A.M.

_____

_____

_____

_____

Friday P.M.

_____

_____

_____

_____

Saturday A.M.

_____

_____

_____

_____

Saturday P.M.

_____

_____

_____

_____

Sunday A.M.

_____

_____

_____

_____

Sunday P.M.

_____

_____

_____

_____

Worksheet 3.7:
Time Pressures Grid

Fill in the parts of your academic, athletic, and personal/social calendar according to the time pressures you feel at that time of the year.

Use + + + + + + for peak activity and time pressures
Use – – – – – – for least amount of activity and time pressures

Mary's time pressures grid would look like this:

	Aug.	Sept.	Oct.	Nov.	Dec.	Jan.	Feb.	Mar.	Apr.	May	June	July
Academic		– – –	+ +	– – –	+ +		–	– – –	+ + –	– – –	– + +		
Athletic		– – –	+ +	– – –	– +	– –	+ + –	+ +				
Personal/ social				+	+ +	+						

Fill in your time pressures grid below to help you identify those periods when you may have the most demands on your academic, athletic, and social life.

	Aug.	Sept.	Oct.	Nov.	Dec.	Jan.	Feb.	Mar.	Apr.	May	June	July
Academic												
Athletic												
Personal/ social												

Now that you see how your peak times line up during the year, you may want to begin planning for those times. One way to do that is to find down times when you can take advantage of having more free time. This is where our final time management skill, *personalizing,* comes in handy. Knowing and using your personal time pattern to advantage is extremely valuable to you as a college athlete. No one's yearly schedule looks exactly like yours. Even athletes on your team will have different schedules if they have different majors than you do. The final exercise in this section will allow you to develop a strategy for dealing with peak pressure times.

In looking at your Time Pressures Grid, you may notice that some peak periods in your athletic life overlap with busy times in your academic life. For example, if you're a baseball player, your final exams and papers may occur during a playoff or tournament. On the other hand, you may notice some down times in February, where both types of pressures are at their lowest. Use these down times to prepare for the peak pressure periods that lie ahead.

On worksheet 3.8, list your down times. Then check off any tasks you can do to prepare for managing the pressure periods better.

As you can see from the cases, exercises, and discussions in this chapter, balancing your athletics, personal life, and academics won't be easy. You can find a balance, however, if you know your priorities, and plan and prepare your personal schedule. We've provided you with some helpful exercises to assist you in your planning. You'll also find that your academic athletic advisor will probably have additional time management planning activities. By using some of these tools, your college years truly will be the best years of your life. Unfortunately, all good things must end, and you'll soon face the challenges of adjusting to life after college.

PREPARING FOR LIFE AFTER COLLEGE

For the vast majority of college athletes, graduation means the end of their formal sport career. Only a few go on to careers in professional sport. We'll address their needs and tasks in the next chapter. The rest of you aren't going to play professional sport because you lack the ability to play at that level or you're in sports that don't have professional opportunities. In either case you can ease your transition out of formal sport participation by preparing in advance for life after college.

To begin your planning, imagine what it will be like after you've ended your college career. Will there be any changes in your friendships, your

Worksheet 3.8:

Using My Down Times

My down times	*My high-pressure times*
Jan. _____	Jan. _____
Feb. _____	Feb. _____
Mar. _____	Mar. _____
Apr. _____	Apr. _____
May _____	May _____
June _____	June _____
July _____	July _____
Aug. _____	Aug. _____
Sept. _____	Sept. _____
Oct. _____	Oct. _____
Nov. _____	Nov. _____
Dec. _____	Dec. _____

Preparation tasks I can do during the down times:

_____ Read books ahead for class

_____ Do research for any papers that are coming due

_____ Organize my room, desk, office

_____ Maintain my fitness level

_____ Visit family, friends

_____ Speak with teachers about my schedule

_____ Write final papers

_____ Shop ahead for clothes, uniforms, presents

_____ Meet with my advisor

_____ Plan my goals for the next semester

_____ Develop my time management plan

sports activities, your family relationships, your finances, your daily routine?

For many of you, the transition out of college will be different from your transitions into high school or college. For the first time you'll need to adjust to a life in which sports don't play such a major role. Those athletes who adjust most easily are those who have achieved their sport goals and had an alternative focus for their energies. During college, these individuals may have had sport as their primary career, but they also had another activity or academic pursuit as their secondary career or interest. Once they graduate, they shift sport into a secondary role and focus primarily on their second career interest. A recent college graduate explained it this way: "I went to school to play volleyball. That is what I loved to do and that's where I put most of my energies. But I also studied and enjoyed being a rehab major. Sure I missed volleyball when I graduated, but now that I am in grad school my studies have become my top priority. Don't get me wrong, I still tear it up in intramurals, but it's not my whole life anymore."

Athletes who don't have interests outside their sport often have difficulty adjusting to life once their formal sport career ends. For example, imagine that you had spent four years of college studying for a career only to find out that a newly created computer wiped out the need for people in that field. If you had nothing to fall back on, you'd probably feel cheated and lost. The same is true of athletics. If you put all your energy into a sport, you may be vulnerable to problems if anything restricts you from participating in that activity.

Even if you still hope to play professionally after college, you may find it helpful to develop a *contingency plan,* an alternative plan that you develop in case your main plan doesn't work. Contingency plans are very helpful for athletes because career-ending injuries and being passed over in the selection process are always possible. Even if you're able to have a professional career, in most sports you'll eventually face retirement at a young age and will probably need to pursue another career. Having an alternative focus may ease your transition when your athletic career ends.

The goal of a career contingency plan is to give you an alternative focus that you can develop while you're still pursuing your college or professional sport goals. You may never be able to find another activity that gives you as much satisfaction as your athletic career, but you may be able to find activities that provide you with some of the same benefits. The next activity, worksheet 3.9, may help you begin to formulate your contingency plan.

Worksheet 3.9:

Developing Your Career
Contingency Plan

A. Think about what you enjoyed and what you disliked about being a college athlete and playing your sport. Now make a list of these positive and negative aspects in the spaces below.

Positive aspects   *Negative aspects*

_____   _____

_____   _____

_____   _____

_____   _____

_____   _____

_____   _____

_____   _____

_____   _____

_____   _____

_____   _____

_____   _____

_____   _____

B. Circle any of the positive aspects that you listed above that you feel would need to be part of an alternative career.

C. Circle any of the negative aspects that you doubt you could tolerate in an alternative career.

D. As you look at your list you'll want to identify a career option that will satisfy many of the circled positives while including few of the circled negatives. To get a better handle on how to identify careers that might best fit your contingency plan, refer to the chapter on career exploration.

Now that you've begun to think about leaving college and the possibility of sport playing a lesser role in your life, remember that ending your college career is a transition and that you've already learned some tools for managing transitions in chapter 1. We've provided you with another copy of Your Game Plan for Transitions to help you plan your strategy for leaving college.

Worksheet 3.10:
Your Game Plan for Leaving College

A. List any concerns that you have about adjusting to life after college.

Physical

1. _____
2. _____
3. _____
4. _____
5. _____

Psychological

1. _____
2. _____
3. _____
4. _____
5. _____

Academic

1. _____
2. _____
3. _____
4. _____
5. _____

Social

1. _____
2. _____
3. _____
4. _____
5. _____

Other

1. _____
2. _____
3. _____
4. _____
5. _____

B. Use circles, squares, or stars to highlight any concerns that might be interrelated.

C. For each area of concern, list any positive coping skills or transferable skill that you used in the past that may help you with this situation.

Area of concern _____

Skills to be used _____

_____

_____

D. For each area of concern, list any support people who may be able to assist you and what kind of support they may provide. Remember that you may have several support people for each area of concern.

Area of concern _____

Name of support persons   *Type of support*

1. _____   _____

2. _____   _____

3. _____   _____

4. _____   _____

5. _____   _____

6. _____   _____

7. _____   _____

8. _____   _____

In the self-exploration chapter, we'll be introducing you to a number of different tools to help you identify your positive coping skills and to assist you in continually upgrading your support team. You can add these skills and resources to your transition game plan to prepare for future transitions.

CHAPTER SUMMARY

The college years are exciting and challenging times for all students. The special challenges that face student-athletes require many adjustments and much support.

From this chapter you should have learned the following:

1. Adjusting to a college life that includes athletics will require many coping skills.

2. You'll make many personal and career identity choices during college.

3. Exploratory behavior is an important way to learn more about yourself.

4. New support people will be available to you in college.

5. Selecting a major will be an important task for you during college.

6. Balancing sports, academics, and social relationships will require much planning and support.

7. You'll have to prepare for life after college during your college years.

Chapter

4

Professional and Elite Athletes

Great athletes are accustomed to performing in the spotlight. Several billion people watch at least some of the athletic events of the Olympic Games. The estimated audience for the Super Bowl every year is over 100 million. But what happens when they turn off the lights and everybody goes home? Even the best athletes rarely survive longer than 10 years at the top of their sport. What happens to them when they stop competing at the elite level?

The contrast can be as stark as that between Joe Gilliam and Fran Tarkenton, two former professional football players. Gilliam was a high-achieving athlete, drafted by the Pittsburgh Steelers in the 11th round in 1972. Only two years later he became the first black quarterback ever to start a regular-season game when he led Pittsburgh over the Colts 30-0 in their opening game. He successfully guided the Steelers to a 4-1-1 start and was rewarded at the season's end when Pittsburgh defeated the Minnesota Vikings to win the Super Bowl. It was the first of two Super Bowl rings Gilliam was to earn with the Steelers. But behavior problems sent his career into a slide. In 1976 he moved to the New Orleans Saints but was dismissed from the team for breaking rules. He attempted a comeback with the U.S. Football League but didn't survive in the new league.

Drug problems surfaced. Gilliam was arrested for possession of drugs, and in 1991 was charged with the armed robbery of a Louisiana restaurant. His only work outside sport was a period as a drug rehabilitation counselor. Today, Joe Gilliam is living on the streets of his hometown in Nashville, Tennessee. He has no job and an uncertain future. Interviewed before the 1996 Super Bowl between the Dallas Cowboys and his old team, the Pittsburgh Steelers, Gilliam commented on his day-to-day philosophy of life: "I take one day at a time, you know. A couple of days, that's too far down the line at this point."

Compare Gilliam's experience with that of former player Fran Tarkenton. He was also a quarterback, playing with the Minnesota Vikings for 18 years before retiring in 1978. During his Hall-of-Fame career he led the Vikings to three Super Bowls, though they lost each one. Even during his playing career, Tarkenton displayed an interest in developing a career other than football. He was an advertising rep for several years, received management training from Coca-Cola Company, and started his own insurance company, all while playing full-time. After leaving football, he founded a computer software company. He didn't find it easy.

"People say to me, 'Oh Fran, you're lucky—you're a big football star and you could start all those businesses,'" Tarkenton once reflected. "I was fortunate in my football career, but I don't know how much that helped me build a software company. When I tried to raise capital I went to bankers and I got zero. I funded the $3 million to get started out of my own pocket, and the most I ever earned in one year as a quarterback was $250,000." By 1986 Tarkenton's company was successful and merged with another company to become Knowledgeware. Tarkenton's stock sold for $2 million.

But business success, like football glory, comes and goes. In 1991 the stock price of Knowledgeware plunged. Tarkenton, as chief executive, found himself the target of lawsuits brought by angry stockholders. In 1994 a rival bought out his company, and Tarkenton was out of a job. But for Tarkenton, a setback means a new opportunity. "I've learned throughout my football and business career that after setbacks—and nothing could set you back more than losing three Super Bowls in front of the entire world—the best thing to do is refocus that negative energy into positive energy." Tarkenton is now busy forming a company that will help small-business people use the Internet, a form of communication that Tarkenton believes is only in its infancy.

CAREER PLANNING FOR ELITE ATHLETES

What makes the difference? Why does one athlete thrive in life after sport, while another constantly struggles? One factor appears to be critical. As we emphasize throughout the book, the athlete who possesses effective life skills will be better able to cope with the challenges of a career outside sport than the athlete who lacks those skills. The self-motivated athlete who is able to set effective goals, develop a career plan, consider a variety of options, and work in a team setting is likely to establish a successful career in a new setting. If your athletic career has moved to the elite level, how can you develop those life skills now so that you'll be ready for the career challenges you'll inevitably face? Here are some ideas based on our career counseling work with many top athletes.

Start Planning for Your Future Career Today

This is a tough one for many elite athletes. Some feel so much pressure that they think they have no time for future career planning.

As a top athlete, you'll often hear advice from those around you. Team owners, coaches, agents, and administrators will often tell you not to worry about the future and to "concentrate 100 percent on your sport." You should realize that they may have selfish reasons for giving this advice. Owners, for example, manage their sports teams as businesses. If teams succeed, their businesses prosper. If teams fail, owners suffer financially. So owners want the athletes on their teams to be single-minded in their pursuit of success. They might not care about your long-term future, which, of course, is critically important to you! Trust yourself most on these issues. *You* are in the best position to look after *your* interests.

What owners, agents, coaches, and others often fail to understand is that athletes will always perform *better* if they take care of their long-term career planning. That's because it's human nature to worry about the future. If you have no plans for your future and no idea what you'll do once you finish in sport, you'll naturally worry about what the future holds. This worry saps your energy and distracts you from what you're doing. It's impossible to be 100 percent focused when you're worried about the future. So taking care of your career plans now will help your sport performance. Top athletes we've counseled have been surprised to see a performance improvement after doing career planning. Sally, a professional tennis player, commented, "It was as if a weight had been lifted off my shoulders. I didn't even realize that the weight was there until it was gone! I'm concentrating on my game and playing so much better now that I've done this career planning with you. I should have done this three years ago!"

So use this book to start developing your own game plan for a future career—today!

Collect Career Ideas

Athletes have some great advantages when it comes to investigating potential careers. Put those advantages to work for you. One advantage you have is that you travel and meet many people in your role as an athlete. Get in the habit of asking people what *they* do for a living. You'll be surprised at the variety of careers out there. Make notes about careers that interest you. If you're interested, ask the person you're talking with, "Where would I go to find out more about how to get the type of job you have?"

Network With Everyone You Meet

When it comes time to start a new career after you retire from top-level sport, it's a great help if people know that you're looking for a new job or a position in a certain field. Everyone who knows about you and knows that you're looking for a position is part of your network. Now is the time to build that network. The more people you have in your network, the faster and easier it will be to find the position you want.

Who can be part of your network? Almost anyone you meet. Certainly family and friends, but also administrators, officials, sponsors, agents, boosters, and backers. You might wish to have a business card printed up with your name and address on it to give to people you meet at events such as fund-raisers and socials. Also, get in the habit of collecting cards from others. When the time comes that you're looking for a job, the extra effort it takes to call those people and tell them what you're looking for can make all the difference between getting your new career off to a flying start or a crash landing.

Apply Sport Skills to Your New Career

We emphasize this point many times in this book. But it's so important that it's worth saying again. The skills that make you a successful athlete can help you be a success in your new career, but only if you recognize your skills and put them to work in your new situation. Think about the following skills, which are all critical in today's business environment. Do you have these skills? Are you working on them?

- Teamwork
- Motivation
- Persistence
- Creative thinking
- Leadership
- Concentration
- Flexibility

Recognize the Many Possible Careers in Sports

When we offer workshops and seminars on career planning to elite athletes, we always ask attendees to tell us about all the types of jobs they can think of in sports. Usually, athletes come up with between 20 and 30 jobs. But there are currently *over 200* types of jobs in the sports area, and new ones are always being added.

Athletes, like all of us, think of the types of jobs they routinely see others performing. Usually they identify jobs such as coach, athletic trainer, agent, sporting goods representative, and team physician. But there are innumerable other career possibilities in the sports world, from facilities manager to team public relations representative to background information researcher for a network or station. Many colleges today offer training and degrees in sports management, administration, and related fields. So before you decide to leave sports behind altogether, check to see if a new role in the sports world might be appropriate for you.

Now that you've started thinking about your future outside top-level sport, let's take an in-depth look at the issues you're likely to face when you decide to retire from elite competition.

HOW WILL YOUR SPORT CAREER END?

While you're competing successfully, you would like to believe that your sport career will end at a moment of your choosing. Most athletes dream of retiring after achieving their goals. Life is full of surprises, and unfortunately the sporting life includes some unpleasant ones. Let's examine the most common ways that your sport career is likely to end. The top ten reasons for retiring from sport are listed in highlight box 4.1.

Highlight Box 4.1

The Top Ten Reasons for Retiring From Sport

1. Achieved sport goals (no challenges remaining)
2. Physical (injuries, declining skills, too much pain)
3. Tired of the lifestyle (travel, no privacy, away from home too much, dealing with the media)
4. Family and friends (need more time for relationships)
5. It was just time to grow up
6. Wanted to go out while on top
7. Tired of all the politics (dealing with management or the sport governing body)
8. Financial
9. Other interests outside sports
10. Bored (tired of playing, not fun anymore)

Injury

This is a frequent circumstance in top-level sport. In some sports serious injuries are almost inevitable. In a retrospective study of their top alpine athletes, the U.S. ski team found that the rate of serious knee injury was 100 percent over four years! Athletes, like any of us, are rarely prepared for serious injury, so the first problem is to deal with the shock of the unexpected setback.

The next step is to decide if you can resume your athletic career after you rehabilitate the injury. This is often a tough decision, and answers are rarely guaranteed. We've worked with many athletes who have made remarkable recoveries and have again competed successfully at the highest levels. But many others have worked just as hard only to find that they've lost the edge they need to be competitive.

Getting Cut

Sport careers often end when a team cuts an athlete or an athlete fails to progress to the next highest level of competition. If you have unrealistic expectations about your sport career, the pain of being cut is likely to be worse. A research study of high school athletes found that 36 percent of black and 14 percent of white athletes who start on teams expected to go on to a career in sports. Contrast this expectation with the finding that in football, for example, less than 5 percent of high school players receive college scholarships to play and, of these, only 1 percent ever have a chance to play in the National Football League. If you don't think about possible alternatives to a career in big-time sport, it will be harder to cope with an unexpected setback, such as not being drafted or not making your sport's Olympic team. The film *Hoop Dreams* relates a real-life story about what athletes go through in such situations. If an athlete doesn't make alternative plans for the development of a career in an area other than sports, transition problems are likely to arise.

One athlete interviewed by sport psychology researcher Patrick Baillie summarized the feelings he experienced after suddenly ending his sporting career: "The most difficult part of retirement was the strange way your sport treats you. One minute everyone involved loves you and includes you. Then, you make a decision to leave the team and they don't even say good-bye. At least at a university, they have a graduation ceremony. As an athlete we give a lot to the sport. They dictate all you do.... A happy retired athlete does a lot more good than a bitter one!"

Age

At some point, even for great athletes like Joe Montana or Rod Carew, age begins to take its toll. The reflexes aren't as sharp as they used to be, and the body doesn't bounce back as quickly as it once did. There comes a time when you have to say good-bye to the sport you love. Depending on the sport, this point may occur at a wide variety of ages. In women's gymnastics, for example, the onset of maturation and the rigors of years of training usually lead top-level competitors to quit before age 20. Yet in some sports, such as shooting or golf, international competitors can still achieve great success in their 40s. Again, the reason for ending your career is not as important as how you react to it. Some athletes accept the decline in skills as inevitable, make other plans, and complete a successful transition to another career. Others, however, fight the process, perhaps by training harder or more "scientifically." They may eventually be forced out of the sport by younger competitors, feeling that they have been betrayed by officials and coaches who don't recognize their continued high level of skill.

Choice

For many athletes there is no sudden decision, voluntary or involuntary, to leave elite sport. Instead, they make the decision gradually, over a long time. The choice to quit usually comes when the top athlete decides that the expected benefits of pursuing some other life activity outweigh the advantages of continued sporting involvement.

The elite female athlete may have fewer choices to continue at the elite-amateur or professional level than her male counterparts. Women have many fewer professional career opportunities in sport than men. Intercollegiate athletic programs employ far fewer women than men as coaches or administrators. This inequitable situation impacts women even earlier, during their athletic careers, since women have fewer roles in sport, despite the passage of Title IX. As an obvious example, an elite male basketball player can expect to make a financially rewarding career from basketball, but few opportunities exist in basketball for the elite female hoops star graduating from college. This situation may slowly change. For example, a top-level women's professional basketball league is currently being discussed. But for many female athletes, the changes won't happen quickly enough.

We've seen many athletes make a very successful transition from sport into another area, especially when they have made the decision carefully. The choice to leave high-level sport participation can lead to great satisfaction and fulfillment in other areas. Athletes who *choose* to retire seem to have an easier time dealing with the transition out of sport than those who are forced to retire. Athletes who choose to retire are often better prepared to deal with the retirement transition because they have considered and planned for life without competitive sport. On the other hand, those athletes who are forced to retire because of injury, getting cut, or management problems are rarely prepared. In addition, most athletes in danger of getting cut will spend more time practicing their sport skills with the hopes of hanging on with a team. Unfortunately, these athletes are then less ready to deal with the mental and social aspects of leaving sport. Often the biggest problem is coming to terms with not reaching your sport goals.

Now that we've taken a long look at why your career might end, let's take a close look at how you might feel once you leave elite-level competition.

COMMON REACTIONS TO ENDING YOUR CAREER

If sport has played a big part in your life for many years, it's unrealistic to expect that you'll walk away from the playing field and never again think about your sporting career. As we suggested earlier, it may be sensible to investigate building a career in sport because you've invested so much time in learning about the field. But even if your postsport career is in another field entirely, you may have to deal with some strong feelings and thoughts about the consequences of quitting elite-level competitive sport. Some athletes we've worked with have described the time after they finish playing as a roller-coaster ride. That ride can last several months or even several years. Realize that such strong emotions are perfectly natural. Here are some common reactions that we've encountered repeatedly in our work with elite athletes.

Sadness Over Loss of the Sport

Many athletes report that they miss all the things their sport career offered: the enjoyment of playing, the status of being a top athlete, the thrill of competition, and the camaraderie of teammates and coaches. A professional ice hockey player described it well: "[I miss] the thrill of playing in front of large crowds and the ego strokes of people wanting your autograph. It's very difficult to replace that rush of scoring a goal, blocking a shot to save a goal, or just being part of a winning team. It would be very difficult to replace that, no matter what we did afterwards."

Loss of Self-Identity

Many top athletes struggle to come up with an answer to the question "Who am I if I can't compete?" For most of their young lives, they have thought of themselves as "Tom the tennis player" or "Kathryn the skater." Now they must move on to a new career and a new identity, or run the risk of being forever stuck in the role of "Tom the ex–tennis player."

Anger at Circumstances Surrounding the End of the Career

An injured athlete might be angry at a player who he or she feels caused the injury. Athletes who have been unexpectedly released might vent their frustration at management.

A major concern you may have to deal with is relating with team ownership, management, or sport governing bodies after your career ends. Many athletes we've worked with have expressed anger and frustration with the "politics" of their sport and the way athletes are treated. In particular, those athletes who were cut from a team often point to the unfairness of the system. It appeared to them that some players received better treatment than others. Some Olympic-level athletes were upset because they felt that athletes from the more glamorous sports received more money and privileges. They felt that they had put out just as much effort and dedication only to be quickly forgotten by their national team governing body when they could no longer compete at international levels of competition. Other athletes became so angry with the sport system that they didn't want anything to do with their sport. They wouldn't even watch it on television.

Loneliness at Separating From Teammates and Coaches

Many retired athletes have told us that they felt alone and misunderstood during their transition out of sport. They said that most of their friends and supporters were people who wanted them to continue to compete. Their friends and supporters couldn't understand why they would want to retire. Thus, many elite athletes felt that no one understood what they went through when they retired from sport.

Fear of an Uncertain Future

Elite athletes tell us that they often feel scared about facing a life after sport. Each sport has its patterns and rhythms. Athletes learn what to expect from year to year, from training and coaching to competition and evaluation. The rewards, from medals to money, and the disappointments, such as media criticism and fan disapproval, can be anticipated. There are no such comforting certainties in the life ahead. The future is now full of unknowns. Athletes commonly go through a period of anxiety as they make the transition from a sporting life to their new career.

Loss of Confidence Toward Life

In their own familiar territory, top athletes feel confident in their abilities. They know how to get the job done in sport. Playing and competing feels comfortable to them, but getting up early to mail out resumes, make phone calls, and go to job interviews feels unnatural. As a result, many athletes doubt themselves in the new situations they meet. They don't know if they have what it takes to make it in the business world or in their new career area.

Frustration Over No Longer Having a Special Status in Life

Often these athletes will think to themselves, "But I'm an elite athlete." Elite-amateur and professional athletes often view themselves as special people. Coaches, fans, and the media reinforce this self-image throughout the athlete's career. If you think of yourself as special, as someone who is an elite athlete, you may have difficulty accepting the thought of changing careers into something that might not be an elite job.

A number of athletes that we've worked with had trouble imagining themselves starting a new career in an entry-level job. They seemed to have forgotten how hard they had to work over the years to reach the level of elite athlete. A career change out of athletics will require you to be willing to learn and grow within a new system. Fortunately, you've developed many skills as an athlete that can make your climb up the success ladder in your new career much easier. We'll help you identify some of these skills in the next chapter.

We've worked with many athletes who shared their fears about putting any effort into planning for the future because the effort might take away from their sport performance. The sport system teaches that you have to devote all your time and energy to your sport if you're going to reach the elite level. This single-minded focus may help you perfect your sport skills but might leave you unprepared for leaving sport. This is especially true if the choice to retire is not yours, but is caused by injury or the team selection process. Many athletes who fear that their skills are declining or that they might not be able to compete with the recruits will spend even more time practicing and conditioning in the hopes of extending their sport career.

It has been our experience that the earlier that you begin to prepare for retirement from sport, the better prepared you'll be to manage it. Giving 110 percent to sport may leave you unprepared to retire and may not even help you improve your overall sport performance. If you're struggling to hang on in your sport, knowing that you've prepared for life after sport can help reduce some of the pressure. As one ski jumper told us, "I'm more confident about the future and I'm hitting a lot more of my jumps. Maybe I'm putting less pressure on myself to be perfect. I don't know for sure, but it feels a whole lot smoother. You know, nothing forced." Maybe spending

2 percent of your time preparing for the future will help you make better career, life, and athletic decisions.

Fear of Being Behind Everyone in the Career World

Another concern we often hear from elite-amateur and professional athletes is the fear that they are years behind their age group with a career. One professional tennis player asked, "How can I possibly catch up to someone my age who has already been working for 10 years?" This athlete was not viewing tennis as her first career. Instead of viewing herself as in the process of changing careers, she expressed anxiety and doubts about her ability to compete with others who had a 10-year head start in the world of work.

As an elite-amateur or professional athlete, you've already established yourself in one career. Now that you're in the process of considering a career change, you need to identify the skills that you've learned through sport and recognize how to use them in different careers. We'll help you do that in the next chapter.

Frustration Over Losing a Sense of Entitlement

Some athletes have been so overprotected and pampered by coaches, fans, and the media that they never worried about developing a career after their playing days were over. The system had previously taken care of these athletes, so they assumed that when they retired from sport someone would just give them a new career. Unfortunately, this isn't usually the case. These athletes later felt that the system used them while they were playing but quickly forgot them when they were no longer needed. Clearly, many elite-amateur and professional athletes receive benefits or perks because of their status.

You should recognize, however, that you may have to work just as hard to identify and secure a new career as you did to gain your status as an elite athlete. It's great to enjoy any perks that may be coming your way, but becoming dependent on the athletic system to continue to care for you may leave you vulnerable to difficulties in coping with the transition out of sport.

Concerns About Managing Money

Money is another concern that you may have to address. If you're making a lot of money, then you need good financial advice to secure your future. The average playing career for athletes in the major sports is only about five years, so you have to plan your investments wisely. In addition, many highly paid athletes become accustomed to the good life and find it difficult to adjust to a lower standard of living.

On the other hand, many athletes who are competing experience pressure because they don't have enough money to continue to pursue their sport goals. They struggle to find ways to make a living while training. Several elite athletes expressed guilt over accepting money from their parents. They could hold only part-time jobs because of the heavy demands of their training schedules and were barely getting by. Other athletes have talked about their need to delay marriage or having children because they didn't make enough money.

Elite athletes have reported these feelings and concerns, and many more, as they move out of sport and into a new phase of their careers. Understand that such reactions are normal. Most athletes go through emotional turmoil after experiencing such a big change in their lives. If you know that your life is about to become a roller-coaster ride, it may make it a bit easier for you cope with the aftershock of the end of your sporting career.

What's the best way to get your life back on track after you stop competing? We'll end this chapter by suggesting some ways in which top athletes can make the career transition process easier.

Highlight Box 4.2

According to the September 30, 1996 edition of the *New York Times*, Bill Carlucci is facing a tough decision. Even though he is just 29 and coming off a bronze medal winning performance as a rower in the Atlanta Olympics, he doesn't know what he'll do. He could spend another four years training for the 2000 Games in Sydney, or maybe it's time to be "a happy person, who has a satisfying job, who has a family, and is not going to get out of bed at 6 o'clock in the morning and put his body through hell for three hours and then come back and do it again, for 10 months, seven days a week." Like many Olympic athletes, Bill is back at home, not much more famous or richer then when he left. He is wondering if he can push himself through the hellish daily workouts for another four years.

On top of everything else, Bill worries about money. Even with the $7,500 prize for winning a medal, several $300 speaking engagements, and $1,500 in endorsements, he will be lucky to make $20,000 for the year. This is far better than the less than $10,000 a year he is accustomed to living on, but a far cry from what other talented, well-educated 29-year-old individuals are earning. At times Bill wonders if all the sacrifices are worth it. Yet he knows that nothing will replace the excitement of competing or the intensity of being a member of the rowing community.

Bill, like many Olympic athletes, is at a crossroad in his career. He is not certain what he will decide about his rowing future, but he does known that someday he "will have to face the inevitable return to being a novice at something."

ENJOYING A SUCCESSFUL TRANSITION FROM SPORT TO THE REST OF YOUR LIFE

One of the reasons we decided to write this book was to relate our experience in helping elite athletes make the transition to life after sport—a transition that you'll someday face. We found that top-level athletes often feel very lonely and unsupported as they make this big move. Two of the programs we've helped develop are the United States Olympic Committee's Career Assistance Program for Athletes (CAPA) and the Ladies Professional Golf Association's Planning for Future Careers Program (PFCP). In both of these programs, athletes have participated in workshops led by career development counselors who specialize in working with elite athletes. The main goals of these workshops have been to provide athletes with a safe place to share with other elite athletes their concerns about leaving sport; to provide them with information about the career development process that you're learning about in this book; and to help them develop a local support system to assist their transition out of competitive sport.

Our experience has taught us what athletes need to make a successful transition. We want to share what we've learned and offer you suggestions based on our experience. Athletes who have participated in our workshops offered the following suggestions when we asked them what advice they would give to other elite athletes.

Talk to Athletes Who Have Left Sport or Are Considering Doing So

During our work with Olympic athletes as part of the Career Assistance Program for Athletes (CAPA), we learned that athletes often need help with expressing their feelings. The athletes we worked with often told us that even though they had many friends, it was still difficult to find anyone who would understand their fears or doubts about retirement.

So, on the one hand, people might not understand what you're going through, but on the other hand, you might be hesitant to tell people what you're feeling. One world-class skier said, "Sports teaches you to tough it out. Telling somebody that you are scared isn't easy." We've learned that many retiring athletes view asking for help as a sign of weakness. At the same time, we know that retiring athletes often have built up many feelings about retirement.

We've also learned that your friends and supporters are probably not going to ask you how you're feeling about retirement because they assume that, as an elite athlete, you have it all together. Thus, many of you would probably benefit from sharing your feelings about retirement with others who would know what you're going through. In our experience with elite athletes, it became clear that the people who are in the best position to understand what you're going through are other retired or retiring athletes.

We learned that many elite athletes must first share their feelings about retirement with others before they can move into the rest of the self-exploration phase of career and life planning. Talking with athletes who have already retired from your sport may not only help you recognize some of the concerns that you face but also help you develop a support system of people who understand your feelings. So find some people in the same boat as you, and talk to them about what you're experiencing.

Talk to a Career Counselor

Another helpful step is to talk to a counselor about what you're going through. In sport, you're often encouraged to tough it out, but this is a time when it does no good to keep your feelings to yourself. Having an understanding person to talk things over with can be a huge help at this time.

A career counselor can be a valuable resource because they specialize in helping people in your situation. Most colleges and universities have counselors, and more sports organizations are also offering career planning assistance to their athletes. Make use of these resources if they are available.

Don't Be Afraid to Ask for Help

Let your family and friends know what's going on. You'll find that people who care about you will be glad to help you if you let them. Unfortunately, we've seen a number of top athletes who have really struggled with starting a new career because they don't admit to anyone that they need help. They are accustomed to being looked up to as a super person, and they think that admitting they need help is a sign of weakness. Instead, they make things tougher for themselves. Don't fall into this trap.

It might be a good idea to stay in touch with your teammates. Suddenly cutting yourself off from sport can make the pain of separation worse. But don't expect that teammates will treat you as they did when you were playing. It's a fact of life that situations change, and coaches and players are likely to have less time to spend with you if you're no longer part of the team.

Plan for the Future

In chapter 1, you looked at your sport life cycle. Each stage within the life cycle contains a beginning, middle, and end. In planning for retirement, you must first determine where you are in your professional or elite-amateur career and when you are most likely to retire. Regardless of the timing of your retirement from sport, you can be actively planning your future career. Many of the activities suggested throughout this book can help you in the career-planning process, but as an elite athlete, you'll have some major career decisions to make at three points in your athletic career: preretirement, retirement, and postretirement. The questions listed below can help you think about decisions you may have to make regarding your employment plans after sport.

Preretirement

1. How can I begin to work toward selecting a future career path now while I'm still competing in my sport?

2. What career areas directly related to my sport, such as coaching or sports marketing, am I interested in exploring while I'm participating in my sport?

3. Are part-time positions or internships available near my training site that might enable me to test the waters or gain experience in a career field outside my sport?

4. Is part-time or correspondence schooling a possibility if I'm unable to attend school full time?

5. Can I make contacts with potential employers as I travel from place to place?

At Retirement

1. How can I best use any financial gains I've made to enhance my future career possibilities?

Worksheet 4.1:

Retirement Planning

1. Where are you in your professional or elite-amateur career?

2. How many years do you have left before you retire?

3. What have you done so far to plan for retirement?

4. When you think about retirement what negative things do you consider?

5. What positive things do you consider?

6. If you've thought about retirement, are there any events that could interfere with your plans?

7. Are there things that you could be doing today that could make your retirement from sport go smoother?

8. Which recently retired athletes could you contact to discuss what it is like to retire?

9. Which active athletes could you contact to discuss your retirement?

10. Does your sport organization provide any career or transition support programs, such as the U.S. Olympic Committee's Career Assistance Program for Athletes or the LPGA's Planning for Future Careers? If your answer is yes, list them.

2. Do I need to jump into a job immediately to support myself? If so, can I find a position that will help me explore career options or build a resume that will help me in later positions?

3. Do I need any emotional support in learning how to adjust to being a rookie in a new career field?

4. How can I use my sport experience and coping skills to deal with my immediate career needs as I am retiring?

5. Do I need to change any of the career plans I made before I retired from sport, such as changing my college major or entering a different training program?

Postretirement

1. How well am I using my athletic experience and networking background to improve my career opportunities?

2. Am I effectively using my sport skills in determining and pursuing my selected career path?

3. How satisfied am I with my current career plan? If I need to make changes, am I using available career resources to help me in my decision making?

4. How well does my current career plan fit with other changes that have been occurring in my life and relationships now that I am retired from sport?

Now that you've examined some general questions about your career-planning process, you need to make a specific plan. Worksheet 4.1 will help you with your planning.

By completing worksheet 4.1, you've begun to think about and plan for your retirement from sport. You've identified some specific people you can contact and some specific actions you can take. The earlier you start planning for your retirement, the more opportunities you have to develop your personal resources and organize your support team.

CHAPTER SUMMARY

When you finally step out of the spotlight, you're entering a brand new world with new challenges and responsibilities. We hope we've shown you what that new world might be like in this chapter. If you know what to expect, it's not as frightening or as intimidating as it seems. Use the Game

Plan for Transitions worksheet in chapter 1 to plan for the end of your sport career and the beginning of your new career.

Give yourself some time to deal with your new role as an ex-athlete. It will take time to readjust. It won't be easy. When you're ready, you'll find the career-planning advice in this book to be very helpful. You might even end up agreeing with one athlete who told us this: "[You] assume that once an athlete has retired from their sport they have retired from all sports. I haven't touched an oar since retirement, but I do a zillion other sports, some competitively, and I work on a program that takes athletes overseas to coach in black townships in South Africa. I doubt any athlete ever retires from sport, just from their sport."

From this chapter, you should have learned the following:

1. You should start your career planning as soon as possible.
2. You can do many things that will facilitate your transition to your next career while you're still participating in your sport.
3. Elite athletes with similar sport experiences can have very different retirement experiences.
4. You need to identify and use your coping skills, your personal resources, and your support team in planning for and growing through your retirement from sport.
5. Elite athletes have special career-planning needs at all phases of their sport careers.

PART II

Exploration and Planning

Chapter

5

Self-Exploration

In this chapter you'll begin the most important, and perhaps most interesting, part of the career-planning process—self-exploration. You may wonder why self-exploration is so important. One reason is that for many people work is drudgery, endured to pay the bills and get to the weekend. These people spend about half of their waking day in a place they don't enjoy. Over time they become dissatisfied and begin to regret lost opportunities. But this is a sacrifice you don't have to make.

Another reason that self-exploration is important is that you are the one making the decisions about your life. Although other people often willingly offer advice, they aren't you, nor will they be walking in your shoes. You're the best person to decide what career is right for you. The better you know yourself, the less tempting it is to follow fads or accept the recommendations of others. Remember, no career is a great career if you don't like it. Let's look at two athletes as they begin the process of self-exploration.

Jeanne, like many seniors in high school, participates in numerous activities. In a typical day, she attends school, goes to basketball practice, makes a quick trip home for supper, and then returns to school for extracurricular events. She wants to go to college next year and play basketball, but she's unsure about selecting a major or making career plans. Her parents think that she should follow her sister and become an accountant. Her best friend is majoring in computer science and told Jeanne that this was a great area for women. A teacher whom Jeanne respects has told her that she's a good writer and should consider a major in English. Personally, Jeanne has always liked history, but she's afraid that there are no jobs for history majors. With advice coming from so many people, Jeanne is confused and nervous about the upcoming year.

Joe is a senior at a nearby college. He is a three-year varsity wrestler who was named to the all-conference team his junior year and is likely to repeat this honor his senior year. Although he's always been a good student, he isn't sure that majoring in business was really the right choice. Some of his classes are interesting, but something seems to be missing. He gets more enjoyment from working with youth at the local community center. But he ruled out a career in recreation because he believed that salaries were low and people would stereotype him as a dumb jock. As he enters his final year in college he's uncertain about his career decisions and somewhat reluctant to start making plans for after graduation.

Both Jeanne and Joe face transitions that will involve major decisions and choices. Daily activities keep them so busy that they feel they have little time to think about themselves and make career plans. The advice of other people and beliefs about certain jobs have created uncertainty. The easy way out for Jeanne and Joe is to let their busy schedules overwhelm them and hope that things will simply fall into place. They risk their future, however, if they don't develop career plans. They probably wouldn't enter a competition without careful training or practice. Although this strategy is occasionally successful in athletics, it's not the one chosen by most coaches or athletes.

LEARNING ABOUT YOURSELF

Like Jeanne and Joe, you may need to spend some time learning about yourself. In particular, there are three key characteristics that you'll want to explore—skills, values, and interests. Skills are necessary for successful work performance. Different work settings require different skills, so you need to know your skills and those required in careers that appeal to you. Skills are the basic assets that prospective workers have to offer employers. Work is competitive, so you'll want to speak the skill language. Everyone has talents, but most of us have difficulty identifying them. You should be comfortable telling potential employers which skills make you well suited for a particular job. It's also important to identify skills you may need to develop to pursue a desired career.

Identifying your skills will make you more competitive in the workplace. Learning about your values and interests will help you choose a satisfying career and lifestyle. Meeting important values on the job and engaging in interesting work will significantly enhance your life and make getting up in the morning more pleasant. Don't underestimate the importance of career satisfaction. Remember, you'll likely spend half of your waking hours at work.

Values are the key factor in determining work satisfaction, so you need to know your values and the rewards provided by different careers. For example, working as a broker on Wall Street might be satisfying for someone who values compensation and adventure, but not for someone who values service to others and job security.

Interests are the key factor in determining work enjoyment, so you need to know your interests and how they match different work environments. If you like to work with your hands and make things, carpentry would be more enjoyable than desk work.

Skills, values, and interests are only one part of self-assessment. Skills, values, and interests develop over time within a broader context called life roles. Jeanne, who is making decisions about going to college and choosing a major, is in a different place than Joe, who is making decisions about choosing a career. Both will be in a different place 10 years from now. Both will be slightly different people with different priorities. Their interests, skills, and values may change as they acquire new life roles and experiences. So, before you begin to assess your skills, values, and interests, it's useful to examine important roles in your life. Looking at your life roles will help you understand why certain things are important, and listing desired roles will help you to set priorities and make plans. This is where you'll begin your self-exploration.

Developing Your Life Roles

Donald Super (1990), a noted career development expert, wrote that our lives are made up of many different roles (e.g., daughter or son, student, athlete, friend, worker, parent, community member, etc.) that become more or less important at different times in our lives. For example, the student role is prominent for most people during adolescence and early adulthood, but becomes less important after that. Through life roles we develop and maintain our skills, values, and interests. For example we often transfer skills learned in school to the work role. Athletes usually learn how to perform under pressure, a skill often required in fast-paced jobs.

We also meet our values through role participation. For example, athletes often value achievement and recognition, which they receive when they perform well. The benefit of holding multiple roles is that no single role becomes overloaded. Different roles meet our many differing needs. It's important to understand that roles change across time as a normal part of development. What is important now may not be important 10 years from now.

In the following exercise we'll ask you to identify important roles that you now hold and important roles that you want to hold in the future. This activity will help you determine which roles permit you to develop skills and express interests and values. In this activity, a circle represents a role and the size of the circle represents the importance of the role. Importance is usually, though not always, related to the amount of time spent in a role. Highlight box 5.1 illustrates Jeanne's life role networks as they are now and as she would like them to be 5 and 10 years from now.

Currently, Jeanne puts much time into being a student, friend, daughter, and athlete. Her roles as a student, friend, and athlete are connected. Many of her friends are also teammates, and she associates some of her athletic activities with being a student. The worker role is minimal because she holds a part-time job as a lifeguard during the summer. She expects her life role network to be different at age 22. Jeanne believes she will be attending school and actively competing in athletics, with her other roles being less important. At age 27, Jeanne hopes to have a full-time job and a long-term relationship. She expects to continue involvement in athletics through recreational sports. The needs that are currently being met through school, athletics, and friends will be met through other roles when she's 27.

Using Jeanne's life role network as an example, draw your current life role network. Try to include all of your major life roles. Circles represent roles and the size of the circle represents the importance of the role. If two roles relate closely, draw the circles close together. Use the space on worksheet 5.1 to draw your life role network as you would like it to be 5 years from now and 10 years from now.

Worksheet 5.1 illustrates three important points. First, roles are important because they meet our needs for love, achievement, and friendship. Second, as we grow and develop, the importance of a role changes. A role may meet many needs during one life stage, then fade in importance later in life. Third, multiple roles provide multiple sources for meeting needs. If you have many ways to meet your needs, the loss or reduction of a major life role won't be disruptive. For example, the end of an athletic career can

Highlight Box 5.1

Jeanne's Role Network

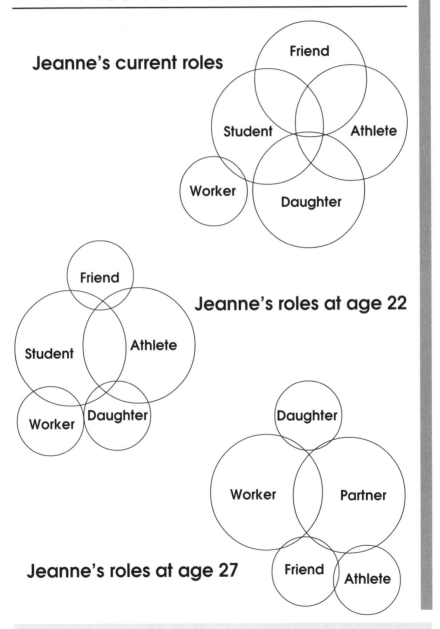

Jeanne's current roles

Friend
Student
Athlete
Worker
Daughter

Friend
Jeanne's roles at age 22
Student
Athlete
Worker
Daughter

Daughter
Worker
Partner
Jeanne's roles at age 27
Friend
Athlete

Worksheet 5.1:

Life Roles

Your current life role network

Your life role network 5 years from now

Your life role network 10 years from now

Life Roles: Some Questions to Ask Yourself

What are your most important life roles? Why are these roles important to you?

What needs are met through each of your life roles?

In what ways will your life be different in 5 years?

In what ways will your most important roles change? As important roles change, how will you satisfy your needs?

How important will your career role be in 5 years? Why? Your athletic role? Why?

In what ways will your life role network be different in 10 years?

How will changes in your life role network influence your career plans?

be buffered by other satisfying life roles, especially the career role. Now that we've addressed the importance of life roles, we can move to three key components of career selection and adjustment—values, interests, and skills.

Values Exploration: What Is Important to Me

Values are the characteristics or ideals that are important in your life. For Joe, giving something back to the community is important. As we noted previously, values differ from interests and skills. Values are what is important to you, interests are what you like to do, and skills are what you do well. You may enjoy badminton and be good at it but not think that it's important. Conversely, you may not enjoy a particular class but still believe that it's important for achieving an education.

Values may relate to lifestyle (e.g., having the opportunity to travel) or more directly to a career (e.g., having a secure job). Not all values are equally important. Some values are more important to you than others. Similarly, what is important to you may not be important to someone else, so you need to look at your values rather than relying on the advice of others.

Jobs also differ in the kinds of rewards they provide. Being an artist may be rewarding for someone who values creativity, whereas being a social worker may be rewarding for someone who values altruism, or helping others. Meeting your values through work is a major source of job satisfaction. In worksheet 5.2, you'll have the chance to think about what's important to you in work and in life. When completing the exercise it's helpful to have an ideal job in mind. If one doesn't immediately come to mind, spend a few minutes daydreaming about your dream job.

In worksheet 5.2, you identified what is important to you—to your core work and lifestyle values. To have a satisfying career and lifestyle, you'll need to find environments or life roles that will reward you in a way that fulfills your values.

Interest Exploration: What I Enjoy Doing

Interests are activities that you enjoy, such as athletics, geography, music, or science. Interests may be broad, like working with people, or more focused, like helping young children. John Holland (1966, 1973, 1985) developed the hexagon model displayed in figure 5.1 on page 106. This model organizes interests into six broad areas that can describe people's work preferences and corresponding occupations. Themes that are adjacent (e.g., realistic and investigative) are more similar than those that are across the hexagon (e.g., realistic and social). Many of the major

Worksheet 5.2:

What Do I Value?

Below is a partial list of lifestyle and work-related values. The separation of work and lifestyle values is for convenience; the two actually overlap. Rate the values listed below by how important each is to you. Think of a work setting that you would enjoy and then rate each value as being very important, moderately important, somewhat important, or not important. Place a check mark in the appropriate column.

Work values categories	Work values	Very important	Moderately important	Somewhat important	Not important
Achievement	Something that makes use of my abilities	___	___	___	___
	Activities that give me a feeling of accomplishment	___	___	___	___
	Developing new skills	___	___	___	___
	Opportunity for advancement	___	___	___	___
Autonomy	Make my own decisions	___	___	___	___
	Work with little supervision	___	___	___	___
	Try out my own ideas	___	___	___	___
	Work independently	___	___	___	___

Work values categories	Work values	Very important	Moderately important	Somewhat important	Not important
Status	Opportunity to supervise others				
	Recognition for the work I do				
	Prestige in the community				
	Persuade others to do something				
Comfort	Pleasant surroundings				
	Good salary and benefits				
	Having paid holidays				
	Not having pressure on the job				
Safety	Being supervised by someone I respect				
	Developing a regular routine				
	Having job security				
	Having clear policies and rules				
Altruism	Helping others work together				
	Helping society and others				
	Working with people				
	Having supportive coworkers				
Others:	_____				
	_____				
	_____				

Lifestyle values	Very important	Moderately important	Somewhat important	Not important
Opportunity to travel				
Leisure involvement and activities				
Living in a certain place or part of the country				
Have many friends				
Close family involvement				
Flexible work schedule				
Financially well off				
Active in community activities				
Active in religious activities				
Others: _____				

Now go through your list and identify your five most important values. Then answer the following questions.

Most important values

1.

2.

3.

4.

5.

Values: Some questions to ask yourself

1. Why are these values important to you?

2. In your current activities (roles) how are these values rewarded?

3. What future activities or roles will allow you to meet these values?

4. What have you learned about your work-related and lifestyle values?

Hexagon Model of Interests

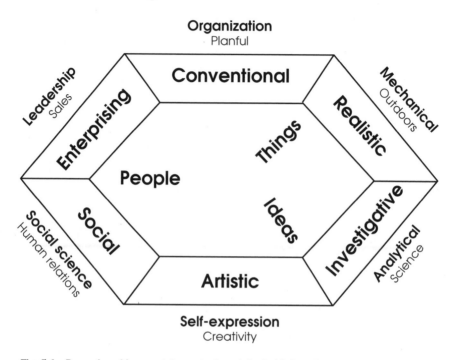

Fig. 5.1 Reproduced by special permission of the Publisher, Psychological Assessment Resources, Inc. from the Self-Directed Search Professional Manual. Copyright 1985 by Psychological Assessment Resources, Inc. All rights reserved.

interest inventories (e.g., Strong Interest Inventory, Self-Directed Search, Career Assessment Inventory) code individuals' responses according to Holland's model. Similarly, over 12,000 occupations have been coded according to Holland's model. Worksheet 5.3 will help you identify your work interests and become familiar with Holland's model, which matches people and occupations based on interest similarity.

The Holland theme descriptions in worksheet 5.3 are rather broad. To help you identify more specific interests, we prepared a list of interest activities grouped within each of the Holland themes. We derived the list from vocational interest research (Campbell, Borgen, Eastes, Johansson, and Peterson, 1968). Read each activity in worksheet 5.4 and decide whether that activity sounds very interesting, moderately interesting, somewhat interesting, or not interesting. Place a check in the appropriate column.

Worksheet 5.3:

Your Work Interests

Read each of the six Holland themes. As you read each theme, underline words that describe you. After you've read each theme, rank order the themes in terms of how well they describe you. The most similar theme should be ranked 1, the next most similar 2, and so on. Most people find that a combination of two or three themes best describes their personality.

Realistic rank: _____

Realistic people like outdoor activities and activities that include working with mechanical or electrical equipment. They prefer working with things rather than people or ideas. They tend to be rugged, athletic, and adventuresome. Typical jobs include forester, carpenter, engineer, and law enforcement officer.

Investigative rank: _____

Investigative people like activities that include investigating, analyzing, evaluating, and solving problems. They prefer working with ideas. They tend to be described as introspective, independent, and curious. Typical jobs include biologist, computer programmer, and mathematician.

Artistic rank: _____

Artistic people like activities that include composing, writing, performing, and self-expression. They prefer working with ideas. They tend to be described as nonconforming, sensitive, and intuitive. Typical jobs include photographer, librarian, author-reporter, and art museum director.

Social rank: _____

Social people like activities that include teaching, explaining, helping, and training. They prefer working with people. They tend to be described as responsible, cooperative, understanding, and concerned about the welfare of others. Typical jobs include school teacher, probation officer, playground director, and practical nurse.

Enterprising rank: _____

Enterprising people like activities that include selling, managing people, giving speeches, and politicking. They prefer working with people. They tend to be described as ambitious, talkative, energetic, and status-conscious. Typical jobs include politician, life insurance agent, personnel director, and corporate executive.

Conventional rank: _____

Conventional people like activities that include typing or filing, organizing, making charts, and keeping records. They prefer working with things or data. They tend to be described as conscientious, practical, preserving, and systematic. Typical jobs include accountant, statistician, telephone operator, and proofreader.

Theme ranked 1: _____

Theme ranked 2: _____

Theme ranked 3: _____

Note: If you want to explore how your interest preferences relate to occupations, you can look through the *Dictionary of Holland Occupational Codes* (Gottfredson & Holland, 1989). Approximately 12,000 occupations are coded according to the RIASEC themes.

After completing worksheets 5.3 and 5.4, you now have a sense of your general work interests as well as specific interests within those broad themes. You've identified your preferences using a model (Holland's model) that links your interests to corresponding work environments. Through these exercises you've identified work and leisure activities that you enjoy. Let's move on to a discussion of skills, a third factor critical in career selection and adjustment.

Skills Exploration: What I Do Well

Skills are developed abilities or strengths. They are the basic qualities that employers look for in prospective employees. It is helpful to organize the many different types of skills into three general categories.

Worksheet 5.4:

Interest Assessment

Interest area	Interest activity	Very interesting	Somewhat interesting	Not interesting
R	Outdoor activities	_____	_____	_____
	Adventure	_____	_____	_____
	Mechanical activities	_____	_____	_____
I	Science	_____	_____	_____
	Mathematics	_____	_____	_____
	Medical service	_____	_____	_____
A	Music/drama	_____	_____	_____
	Art	_____	_____	_____
	Writing	_____	_____	_____
S	Teaching	_____	_____	_____
	Social services	_____	_____	_____
	Team sports	_____	_____	_____
E	Public speaking	_____	_____	_____
	Law/politics	_____	_____	_____
	Merchandising/sales	_____	_____	_____
C	Office practices	_____	_____	_____
	Detail-oriented activities	_____	_____	_____

Questions

1. Look down the "very interesting" column. Do your check marks cluster in certain areas? Which ones would you consider in a job? Which ones are recreational interests only?

2. What current activities best fit your interests? Are there activities that you haven't yet tried but would like to try?

3. What is it about your top interest areas that makes them interesting?

4. What new activities do you want to try? What interest area would they belong to?

Note: If you checked a number of different activities you may have diverse interests. That's OK, but it may mean that you'll want to look more carefully at your values and skills to help you narrow your career choices.

Content Skills

Content skills develop from specific acquired knowledge or training necessary to perform in certain occupations. For example, sports agents need to know how to negotiate contracts, and this requires specific knowledge of laws and contracts.

Adaptive Skills

Personal qualities that help you adapt to different situations are called adaptive skills. We often think of them as personality traits. Characteristics such as motivation, initiative, and persistence are adaptive skills that help people succeed in different occupations.

Transferable Skills

Abilities learned in one role that can be used in another role are called transferable skills. Athletes sometimes believe that they have few skills beyond those learned in athletics. However, many of the skills learned as an athlete transfer to other roles. Some of these skills are conceptual, such as the ability to develop complex training and performance strategies, whereas others are more adaptive, such as dedication and discipline. Working effectively with teammates is a skill that can translate to working effectively with coworkers.

Identifying skills is sometimes difficult because we've been taught not to brag or toot our own horn. But identifying skills is crucial for career planning. The process builds confidence (yes, everyone has many skills) and helps people put their experiences into words employers can understand. The following exercises (worksheets 5.5, 5.6, 5.7) will help you identify content, adaptive, and transferable skills. By completing these exercise you'll have the beginning of an impressive skills vocabulary. This vocabulary will help you communicate with prospective employers and allow you to effectively label and categorize future activities and experiences.

Worksheet 5.5:

Rating My Work Content Skills

You can also arrange skills according to the Holland hexagon that was introduced in the previous section. Listed below are a number of content skills grouped according to the Holland categories. Think about success-ful experiences that you've had in school, work, athletics, or extra-curricular activities. Then check whether you've developed this skill to a great extent, some extent, little extent, or no extent.

Developed skills	Great extent	Some extent	Little extent	No extent
Realistic				
Operate machines				
Repair equipment				
Construct/build things				
Physical stamina				
Assemble things				
Work with tools				
Visualize shapes and dimensions				
Estimate physical space				
Investigative				
Carefully analyze a problem				
Accurately compute problems				
Understand scientific principles				
Solve puzzles				
Research new topics				
Conduct data analyses				
Read graphs and charts				
Artistic				
Write stories, poetry				
Design new ways of doing something				
Read or perform music				

Developed skills	Great extent	Some extent	Little extent	No extent
Express ideas or information in written form				
Draw or paint				
Decorate (i.e., interior design)				
Speak foreign languages				
Act or perform in public				

Social

Advise or counsel people				
Arrange social activities				
Listen to others				
Mediate between people				
Teach or coach				
Converse comfortably with many people				
Work effectively on a team				
Get along with different people				
Work with children				
Encourage and support others				

Enterprising

Collect money				
Persuade others				
Manage or supervise others				
Speak publicly				
Raise funds				
Sell products				
Run meetings				
Debate topics				
Understand laws and contracts				
Find bargain buys				

Conventional

Keep records or books				

Developed skills	Great extent	Some extent	Little extent	No extent
Check accuracy of work (proofread)	___	___	___	___
Handle detail work	___	___	___	___
Plan and organize personal activities	___	___	___	___
Follow procedures	___	___	___	___
Copy information accurately	___	___	___	___
File materials	___	___	___	___
Prepare budgets	___	___	___	___
Type or word process	___	___	___	___

Work content skills: Some questions to ask yourself

1. In which areas (e.g., realistic, investigative) have you developed the most skills?

2. Are these skill areas the same as your favorite interest areas?

3. What new skills would you like to develop? In which group would they belong?

Worksheet 5.6:

Adaptive Skills Exercise

Below you'll find traits that characterize people. Circle the 20 traits that best describe you.

aggressive	bold	cooperative
cheerful	conscientious	cordial
candid	considerate	courageous
creative	daring	diligent
efficient	energetic	ethical
friendly	generous	good-humored

honest	innovative	intelligent
independent	judicious	kind
logical	loyal	modest
mature	methodical	neat
open-minded	organized	optimistic
outgoing	persuasive	persistent
punctual	patient	perceptive
relaxed	reasonable	respectful
reliable	resourceful	sincere
sociable	smart	studious
truthful	tactful	understanding
unselfish	versatile	warm

Some questions to ask yourself

1. How do the traits that you circled help you adapt to new situations?

2. Which adaptive skills do you use most often in athletics?

3. How will these skills help you in a work setting?

Worksheet 5.7:
Transferable Skills

The following transferable skills exercises were designed for Olympic athletes who are approaching athletic retirement or have recently retired. The exercises will help you identify your sport-related skills and translate them to work-related skills.

Section 1: This section contains questions that will help you identify personal characteristics and skills you've developed through sport participation. Please list at least five answers to the following questions:

Part A

1. What personal qualities and characteristics do you think coaches and teammates look for in athletes?

2. What other personal qualities and characteristics do you think are important for athletic achievement?

3. What personal qualities and strengths have helped you succeed in sport?

4. What have you learned from your extensive precompetition practice experience?

5. What have you learned from competitive situations?

Part B

1. Review your responses to numbers 1 and 2 in part A. Describe how these may be similar to and different from what employers look for in prospective employees.

2. Again, review your responses to numbers 1 and 2 in part A. How might these qualities and characteristics be important for career development and life decisions?

3. Review your response to number 3 in part A. How might these qualities and strengths be important for your career development and life decisions?

4. Review your responses to numbers 4 and 5 in part A. How might you apply what you've discovered to areas of your life outside sport?

5. How do you think the concept of teamwork might be applied to work settings? How might it be especially beneficial in a work setting?

Section 2: This part of the exercise will help you identify skills that might be transferable to nonsport settings. For each category, please check all that apply.

	Important for succeeding in sport	Important for succeeding in the workplace	Skills I have	Skills I need to develop	Comments
1. Making a commitment and sticking with it					
2. Learning to win and lose					
3. Working with people I don't necessarily like					
4. Learning patience					
5. Becoming disciplined					
6. Being fit					
7. Learning respect					
8. Learning to be creative					
9. Learning to take orders					
10. Learning self-control					
11. Learning communication skills					

12. Learning drive and dedication; pushing myself to the limit _____ _____ _____ _____

13. Learning my limitations _____ _____ _____ _____

14. Learning to compete without hatred _____ _____ _____ _____

15. Accepting complete responsibility for my behavior _____ _____ _____ _____

16. Learning to commit a great deal of time and effort _____ _____ _____ _____

17. Ability to accept criticism and feedback in order to learn _____ _____ _____ _____

18. Learning to take risks _____ _____ _____ _____

19. Developing a sense of accomplishment _____ _____ _____ _____

20. Learning to evaluate myself _____ _____ _____ _____

21. Learning to be flexible _____ _____ _____ _____

22. Learning to perform under pressure _____ _____ _____ _____

PUTTING IT ALL TOGETHER: DEVELOPING YOUR PERSONAL PROFILE

After completing the values, interests, and skills assessments you've undoubtedly learned new things about yourself. But you may feel that you're working on a puzzle whose pieces you still need to put together. This part of the self-exploration chapter will help you complete the puzzle to develop a complete and integrated picture of your values, interests, and skills.

After Jeanne worked through the values, interests, and skills exercises, she developed her personal profile. Some of her responses are listed in highlight box 5.2.

Highlight Box 5.2

Personal Profile

Values

Career: achievement, autonomy, independence, creativity, variety
Lifestyle: have friends, travel

Interests

Recreation: basketball, music, reading biographies
Career: writing, music, outdoor activities, law/politics, adventure

Skills

Adaptive: reliable, hardworking, creative, patient, intelligent, diligent, perceptive
Transferable: disciplined, self-control, perform under pressure
Work content: research new topics, write stories, listen to others, teamwork, plan activities

She then used these lists to create an ideal job that met her most important values, interests, and skills:

My ideal job would involve some outside work and some desk or library work. I would make up my own schedule and there would be a lot of variety in what I do. I would study history and go out to visit historic sites. I would like to write about what I study. I could see working in a museum and going out to investigate events and collect historic pieces. I could then write stories for the museum displays, or maybe write articles for history journals and magazines.

Now that you've seen how Jeanne put her self-assessment information together, it's time to develop your personal profile using worksheet 5.8. Your personal profile will give you ideas about what characteristics to look for in prospective jobs and careers. In chapter 6, you'll learn about career exploration by comparing your profile to different work settings. Remember, different jobs reward different values, interests, and skills. Knowing what you want will help you get the career that's right for you.

Worksheet 5.8:

Personal Profile

Use your responses from worksheets 5.2 through 5.7 to create a list of your most important values, interests, and skills.

Values

Career: _____

_____

_____

Lifestyle: _____

_____

_____

Interests

Recreation: _____

_____

_____

Career: _____

_____

_____

Skills

Adaptive: _____

_____

Transferable: _____

_____

Work content: _____

_____

Creating an Ideal Job

Use the information from your personal profile to create an ideal job (i.e., what your ideal job would look like). You may want to use the following guidelines to help you get started.

A. Choose the five characteristics on your personal profile that are most important to you. Label them as interests, values, or skills (e.g., working with people—interest; achievement—value).

1.

2.

3.

4.

5.

B. If you don't have a mix of skill, interest, and value characteristics, add a few characteristics so that you have at least one of each.

1.

2.

3.

C. Decide whether you want to use your top interests, values, and skills in the work role rather than other life roles.

My ideal job would be the following:

CHAPTER SUMMARY

Self-assessment is a critical part of life and career planning. Your life roles provide you with opportunities to meet important needs. Life roles are also the context within which you develop interests, values, and skills. Identifying current and anticipated life roles will help you develop a framework for life planning. Identifying your interests, values, and skills will help you develop a framework for career planning. You'll use this framework as you research different careers in the next chapter.

In this chapter, you should have learned the following:

1. Your life role network shows you how each role meets different needs and that your roles will probably change over time.

2. Values, interests, and skills are important characteristics in determining what to look for in a career. Values are qualities that are important to you, interests are activities that you enjoy, and skills are what you do well.

3. Having a career that meets your value, interest, and skill preferences is likely to enhance both your career and life satisfaction.

REFERENCES

Campbell, D.P., Borgen, F.H., Eastes, S., Johansson, C.B., & Peterson, R.A. (1968). *Journal of Applied Psychology Monographs*, **52**, No. 6, Part 2.

Gottfredson, G.D. & Holland, J.L. (1989). *The dictionary of Holland occupational codes* (rev. Ed.). Odessa, FL: Psychological Assessment Resources.

Holland, J.L. (1966). *The psychology of vocational choice*. Waltham, MA: Blaisdell.

Holland, J.L. (1973). *Making vocational choices: A theory of careers*. Englewood cliffs, NJ: Prentice-Hall.

Holland, J.L. (1985). *Making vocational choices: A theory of vocational personalities and work environments*. (2nd Edition). Englewood Cliffs, NJ: Prentice-Hall.

Super, D.E. (1990). A life-span, life-space approach to career development. In D. Brown, L. Brooks, and Associates, *Career choice and development*. (2nd Edition), 197-261. San Francisco: Jossey-Bass.

Career Exploration

$\mathbf{A}$lthough you may know a great deal about yourself, you may have limited knowledge about occupations. If this is the case, two common problems in selecting an appropriate career are likely to occur. The first is limiting your career choices because you aren't aware of all available options. The second problem is basing your beliefs about a particular career on imagination or hearsay rather than fact. Secondhand information or personal beliefs about a career don't necessarily match reality. It's wise to test your perceptions about a career before investing time and energy in job training and preparation.

In this chapter we'll teach you how to avoid problems that might result from limitations in your knowledge of occupations. You'll learn a model of career exploration, factors that can impede your exploration, how occupations are organized, and strategies for gathering career information.

EXPLORING CAREERS

Before discussing career exploration, we need to review the differences between jobs, occupations, occupational fields, careers, and career change. In this book, we use the term job to refer to a specific type of work done in a specific setting. You may have already held several jobs, such as lifeguard, waiter, or sales clerk. An occupation is a bit broader and includes similar tasks that could be performed in different situations. For example, psychologists might do test-interpretation work for business and industry, school systems, the military, or the government. An occupational field is even broader and includes related occupations. The field of medicine, for example, includes occupations such as physician, nurse, medical technologist, and medical researcher.

A career is somewhat different from the other categories. A career is series of jobs that leads to a planned or purposeful outcome. It involves an individual's work history, and can include different jobs, occupations, or even occupational fields. For example, if you had a career goal to own and manage a used sports equipment store, you might take jobs in sales, management, and bookkeeping to learn how to run a business. To make contacts and stay visible in the athletic world, you might work part-time as a coach. Although these jobs are in different occupations, they each fit into your career development plan by giving you the skills and training to prepare you to reach your career goal. A career change is a move from one occupational field to an unrelated field. For example, a switch from engineering to elementary education would be a career change.

Career exploration is like an expedition into a new region of the world. It can be very exciting, but you need to know your strengths and limitations and have a good working map of the territory. Without this information you could get lost, have difficulty communicating, or have problems adjusting to the new culture. You have already begun self-exploration in the previous chapter. Now it's time to use this information to help you navigate the world of work.

We have prepared a framework to teach you the skills you'll need to engage in career exploration. This framework will help you organize the information that you gather. As you learned in the previous chapter, you have certain interests, values, and skills. The world of work, just like the world of sports, contains occupations that differ in settings, rewards, and skills. Your goal is to explore different occupations and career paths and narrow the field to those that best match your preferences. The career exploration process is a cycle in which you gather occupational information, evaluate what you learn about different occupations, and make decisions. You repeat the process until you arrive at a specific occupation that best meets your current needs and best matches your values, interests, and skills. After you've selected the best option, you'll be ready to move from exploration to job acquisition, that is, learning specific job search strategies that will help you secure the occupation of your choice. We'll cover job search strategies in chapters 8, 9, and 10.

Figure 6.1 diagrams the career exploration process. This figure will serve as your guide to understanding how to gather occupational and career information.

As you can see from figure 6.1, career exploration is a continual process of gathering information about yourself, careers, occupations, and jobs so that you can find the best fit between your personal preferences and a work setting. Remember that a career develops over time. You may choose an entry-level job that isn't particularly interesting because it will give you the skills necessary to move to a more satisfying job. Both jobs will contribute to your career development.

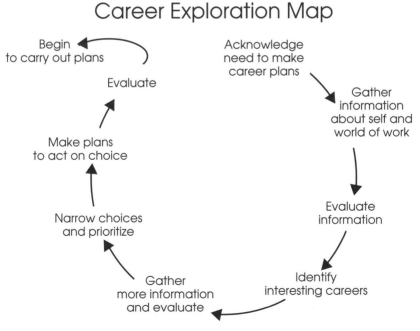

Career Exploration Map

Begin to carry out plans

Evaluate

Make plans to act on choice

Narrow choices and prioritize

Gather more information and evaluate

Acknowledge need to make career plans

Gather information about self and world of work

Evaluate information

Identify interesting careers

Fig. 6.1.

Person–Job Fit

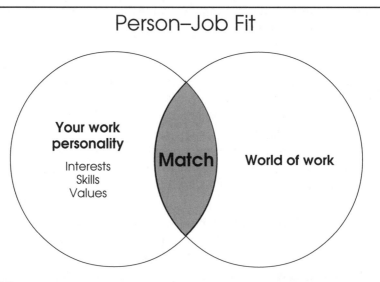

Fig. 6.2.

Your Personal and Career Profile

Fig. 6.3.

Unfortunately, seldom do a person's personal preferences match perfectly his or her career, so you should identify personal characteristics your work role must satisfy. Figure 6.2 illustrates this point.

As you can see from the diagram, your personal profile and career profile overlap. Your happiness in a work setting will typically correspond to how well your values, interests, and skills match the characteristics of a job. You've identified many of your most important values, interests, and skills in the personal profile that you completed in the previous chapter. Your ideal career will enable you to satisfy, directly or indirectly, the most critical requirements of your personal profile. At the very least, your career should overlap with the "musts" of your personal profile, as shown in figure 6.3.

Before you start the career exploration process, you need to be aware of some of the hazards that can block your path.

HURDLES AND BIASES

Over the years we form impressions about many occupations. Perhaps you learned that accountants are boring, mechanics are men, and teachers aren't paid very well. These beliefs can turn you off before you consider a career that might be a good fit. Perhaps you developed beliefs through your family. Maybe your favorite uncle, a successful businessman, was outgoing and charming. You doubt that you could ever match his charisma; therefore, you could never be successful in business. Buying into these myths will limit your career options

Myths or false beliefs aren't the only way we limit our ability to explore careers. Sometimes expectations from others get in the way. A college football player came in for career counseling after he had been struggling in his preengineering courses. He indicated that his father and three older brothers were all engineers. Being an engineer was an unspoken family tradition that would be tough to break. His interests, values, and skills were more in line with business, but he was still reluctant to consider business as a career. Surprisingly, he didn't know why he was hesitant to consider any career other than engineering. The expectation that he follow in the footsteps of his father and brothers was very strong even though he wasn't fully aware of it.

Another young football player faced quite different expectations. He had grown up in a tough urban neighborhood and knew that few people from his area ever made it in professional careers. He figured that if he didn't do well in football, he had little chance of being successful in another profession. His family and friends held high expectations for him in football but didn't encourage him in areas that they felt might take away from his chances of becoming a professional athlete.

A female basketball player came in for career counseling because she was feeling confused about her future. She was doing very well as a premedicine major, but was questioning whether she wanted to follow her father into the medical field. She remembers that her father was never home when she was growing up, and she didn't want to do the same thing to her family. She wanted to transfer into a different major even though she was doing well and enjoying what she was learning. In this case, she didn't want to follow in her father's footsteps, even though medicine may have been a good career fit.

We also have expectations of ourselves. Athletes are accustomed to performing well. Sometimes they carry this standard of excellence with them into career exploration. Athletes may look only at jobs that they are familiar with or confident about, usually careers in athletics. They are confident in their ability to coach, for example, but less sure about careers in which they have no experience. It's easy to forget that developing a career is just like beginning a new sport. It requires practice and new steps may feel awkward at first.

Beliefs, myths, and expectations of others and ourselves aren't always obvious, but they can affect how we make career decisions. The best way to find a satisfying career is to start with the largest possible pool of careers and systematically narrow it down by eliminating occupations that don't fit your profile. We'll teach you how to develop a pool of possible careers in the sections that follow.

ORGANIZING THE WORLD OF WORK

The first step in creating your pool of possible careers is to understand how occupations are organized. There are over 20,000 occupations in the United States, so you may need some help in understanding how careers relate to one another.

Occupations are typically organized by skill level and field. Level refers to the amount of responsibility and skill needed to carry out job requirements. Skills can be grouped into three categories depending on whether they concern data, people, or things. In the *Dictionary of Occupational Titles,* each occupation description includes a list of necessary skills related to data, people, and things. Each skill is coded according to a hierarchy from basic to advanced skills. For example, proofreading a chart for accuracy is a basic data skill whereas integrating and analyzing information to discover facts is a high-level data skill. An inventory clerk position would require basic data skills; a research scientist position would require advanced data skills.

Occupations are also organized by field or areas of interest and competencies. The hexagon used to arrange interests in the previous chapter can also be used to group occupations, as shown in figure 6.4.

Occupations can be organized in many ways, but most career information books and resources use some variation of occupational level and

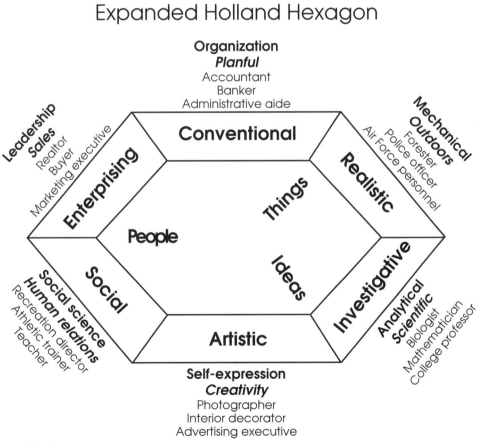

Fig. 6.4.

field to present material. By understanding how occupational information is presented, you'll know where to look and what to ask. You can find useful information in libraries, newspapers, magazines, and, certainly, through people. We encourage you to use all the resources that you have available.

Next, we want to review a couple of efficient career exploration strategies. We'll introduce written resources that provide a summary of work settings. We'll discuss more specific resources and, finally, talk about informational interviews and shadowing.

STRATEGIES FOR CAREER EXPLORATION

Some people have a specific career path in mind when they begin career exploration. They may not know much about a certain career, but something about it sounds interesting. Or they may have a specific career path in mind because of the expectations of others. For example, as one athlete put it, "Both my parents are teachers and I knew from day one that I was going to be a teacher."

Other people have ideas about what they like but don't know which careers interest them. Athletes will often say that they want to work in a job related to sports, but they aren't sure which athletic careers interest them.

These two categories represent two types of career exploration problems. In the first category the athlete has identified a possible career path but hasn't carefully matched it with personal preferences; in the second category the athlete has identified personal preferences but hasn't matched them with a career path.

In the first situation, you should gather information about a specific career and then go back to your personal profile to see if this career overlaps with your most important values, interests, and skills. This quick and easy approach is useful if you've always dreamed about a certain occupation or career path. Although your intuition about a dream career may be accurate, you should check the facts. You may also need to gather additional information, such as the type and level of training that you would need to enter this occupation.

In the second situation, you'll start with your personal profile to find areas that interest you, such as technical/mechanical. You then use this information to begin identifying occupations that match your interests. You may find that groups of occupations are related to one another. If so, you'll have many more choices once you start working in a certain field.

Category #1: I Know What Career I Like, I Just Don't Know What People in That Career Do

As the title suggests, you may have a few careers or occupations in mind but need more information about them. The first strategy we describe isn't as thorough as the second one, but it's useful for those who want quick answers to specific questions. This strategy involves going to a library or guidance counselor's office and browsing through a copy of a general occupational information book, such as the *Occupational Outlook Handbook, The Guide for Occupational Exploration,* or the *Dictionary of Occupational Titles* (this one is less user-friendly than the other two).

Let's work through an example of this process. A young woman interested in being a sports broadcaster went to the school library and got a copy of *Occupational Outlook Handbook.* In the index she found the term sportscaster, with a reference to radio and television announcers and newscasters. She read about the nature of the work, working conditions, avenues of employment, training, other qualifications, advancement, job outlook through the year 2000, average annual earnings, related occupations, and sources of additional information. She checked her self-assessment profile and found that her interests in art and self-expression, her values for achievement, and her skills in high school drama all fit this career. Although the field sounded fascinating, she learned that competition was keen and began to question her ability to get a position. She read suggestions on how to prepare for and advance in this career. She also read about related occupations. She noticed that radio and television announcers and newscasters were listed under communications occupations along with public relations specialists, reporters and correspondents, and writers and editors. She read through these career descriptions as well. They sounded interesting but not as good as broadcasting. She then decided to write for further information using references listed under sources of additional information.

Through this process the student was able to gather information that would help her make a better decision. Although she discovered that her values, interests, and skills matched up well to her selected career, she now had to decide if she were willing to invest a lot of time and energy pursuing a career that might have limited job opportunities. We'll show you how to address decisions involving risk taking in the next chapter, but now let's move on to the second career exploration problem category.

Category #2: I Know What I Like but I Don't Know What Career I Want

Your self-assessment profile, which includes your major interests, values, and skills, will help determine where to begin gathering occupational information and how to evaluate it. For the sake of convenience we'll use one book, *The Enhanced Guide for Occupational Exploration (GOE)*, as an example of how occupational information is presented. This reference describes 2,500 occupations, organized according to 12 interest areas. These areas correspond closely to the ones on your hexagon:

- Realistic—plants and animals, protective, mechanical, and industrial
- Investigative—scientific
- Artistic—artistic
- Social—accommodating, humanitarian, physical, performing
- Enterprising—selling, leading, influencing
- Conventional—business detail

Within each of the 12 interest areas are lists of more specific occupational areas. To show you how this process works, let's use an example of a young man with social interests.

You'll recall from the previous chapter that Joe was feeling uncertain about his decision to major in business because he gained more satisfaction from working with youth at a community center than from his business courses. Initially, he had ruled out recreation work because he didn't want to be perceived as a dumb jock. But his uncertainty influenced him to explore his career possibilities. He began by identifying in his personal profile interests, values, and skills that he enjoyed using. Many of his interests fell in the social category. He then went to *GOE* and looked up the interest area called humanitarian. The definition of humanitarian is almost identical to the definition of social interests. Within this broad area he read about career fields related to helping others, such as social services. Joe learned about what kind of work social service professionals do, what types of skills they need, and how to prepare for this profession. He answered some questions to get a better idea of whether this field was for him (e.g., "Do others come to you for advice?"). Another section described a few points that those interested in social services should consider. For example, social service professionals must deal with much personal information and must attend continuing education to stay current in the field. Within the field of social services, Joe read about specific career areas such as counseling and social work. The counseling and social work career area includes occupations such as case aide, case worker, community worker, probation and parole officer, and counseling psychologist. All of these occupations deal with counseling and social work; however, they differ in specific job functions, level of training needed, and populations served. They are in the same field but at different levels.

Joe also found information in *GOE* that is helpful to people who aren't sure how much education they want to obtain, to readers who want to know all the occupations in a certain industry, and to those who want to get a better idea of the skills required in different occupations. Joe read the list of occupations by level of training because time spent in school was an important consideration for him. He decided that as long as it would meet his interests and values, he would rather pursue a lower level job that required less training than a higher level one.

As Joe read through the different occupations, he jotted down the names of the ones that sounded interesting on the side of his personal profile sheet. He then reread those descriptions and placed check marks where the occupation matched his interests, values, and skills. After an hour of work he had learned about several interesting careers and compared them with his preferences.

BEGINNING YOUR CAREER EXPLORATION

Like Joe, you may want to begin your career exploration. We've provided some exercises and activities on worksheet 6.1 that will guide you in your search.

Getting More Career Information: Informational Interviews

Learning to use the library is one of the most important skills you can acquire in career exploration. However, we aren't asking that you confine yourself to being a bookworm. An exciting and interesting way of gathering career information is talking to people you know or meet about their careers. You talk to your teachers almost every day. But have you ever asked them what they like and dislike about teaching? Others who can provide career information are neighbors, community members, and

Worksheet 6.1:

Career Exploration Exercise

In this exercise you'll develop a career profile grid and evaluate at least three occupations according to your career preferences. Use the grid provided below to list your most important interests, values, and skills. These would be those items on your "must" list in your career profile. Then go to a career information resource, such as *The Guide for Occupational Exploration*, the *Occupational Outlook Handbook*, or one of those listed in appendix A. Look up occupational areas that sound interesting and read about the careers within those areas. Write down three occupations. Read the career descriptions carefully and decide whether those careers match your most important interests, values, and skills. Place a check under every matching interest, value, and skill. For example, if you were reading about coaching, your grid might look like this.

Most important interests, values, and skills

Occupation	1. Teaching	2. Job security	3. Leadership	4. Variety	5. Achievement
Coaching	X		X	X	X

Create your own job grid

List your most important interests, values, and skills in the space provided.

Occupation	1.		2.		3.		4.		5.	

relatives. A side benefit from these interactions is that you often learn something new about people in your life.

The purpose of an informational interview is to gather information, not to get a job. Informational interviews can be informal or formal. You generally conduct an informal informational interview with someone you know in a casual setting, such as interviewing your next door neighbor at home. This is a good way to develop your information-gathering and interviewing skills in a nonthreatening environment.

A formal informational interview involves setting up an appointment with someone you want to talk to but may not know personally. A formal interview is necessary if you don't know anyone in a particular field. You may need to go through the yellow pages or ask family and friends to identify an appropriate person. If you are an athlete who has traveled extensively, you may want to contact people you've met during your travels. If you're still participating in sport and traveling, make it a point to collect business cards from people you meet. Although it may seem presumptuous to call a person you don't know and ask for an interview, most people are willing and even flattered to talk about their career if you explain your purpose. These steps will guide you through a formal informational interview.

Contacting the Person

1. Before you phone or write for an appointment, find out the name and title of the person with whom you want to talk.

2. Introduce yourself and, if you were referred, include the name of the person who referred you.

3. Explain that you are seeking an informational interview to learn more about a particular career. Clearly state that you aren't seeking a job interview.

4. Ask for a 20-minute appointment at a time convenient for that person. You may want to offer to take the person to lunch.

5. If the person isn't available to meet with you, ask if he or she could recommend someone else with whom you could talk. Also, ask if you could use his or her name when contacting that person.

Preparing for the Interview

1. Go to the library and conduct an occupational information search for background about the career.

2. If possible, try to learn about the company or organization for which this person works.

3. Prepare four or five open-ended questions (e.g., those that start with "What" or "Why") that will allow the person to speak beyond yes or no answers. Sample questions include the following:

   a. What do you like best about your job? Least?

   b. What skills are critical for your job?

   c. How much training or education is needed for a career like yours?

   d. What is the salary range for someone in this field?

   e. What are the opportunities for advancement?

   f. What is the job market for people in this career?

   g. What else could I do to learn more about this career?

   h. What are the most important things I need to know about this career?

4. Select professional clothing and make sure that you know how to get to the place where you agreed to meet. Missing an appointment because you got lost isn't professional.

Conducting the Interview

1. Arrive a few minutes before your scheduled appointment.

2. Introduce yourself, thank the person for taking the time to talk with you, and explain your purpose again.

3. Ask the person whether he or she would be comfortable with your taking notes.

4. Use a comfortable, competent, confident, and professional style. Make eye contact and be a good listener.

5. Observe this person's work setting and his or her style of communicating. Is it formal or informal? Technical? Is this a place where you would like to work? Is this a person you would want to be like or work with?

6. End the interview on time and thank the person for speaking with you. If appropriate, you may want to ask the person for his or her business card.

Following the Interview

1. Send a thank-you note within one day following the interview.

2. Write down your observations and place them in your career information file. Go over the notes you took during the interview

and jot down any impressions or reactions. Keep these notes in an informational interview notebook or file. An example of an informational interview file sheet is shown in worksheet 6.2.

Worksheet 6.2:
Informational Interview File Card

Interview: Formal _____   Informal _____

Date: _____

Person interviewed: _____

Person's title: _____

Person's address: _____

Phone: _____

Interview summary: _____

_____

_____

_____

_____

_____

_____

What you learned or your reactions: _____

_____

_____

_____

_____

_____

_____

_____

_____

_____

Shadowing and Internships

Shadowing is a term that refers to following and observing someone on the job. Being able to follow someone as he or she performs daily tasks is an exciting way to learn about a job. Many of the suggestions we offered for conducting an informational interview also apply to shadowing. Many people are willing to let you observe them at work as long as you don't cause inconvenience or distraction. Of course, aspects of some occupations aren't open for observation. For example, when a lawyer speaks with a client the meeting may need to be confidential. Portions of most occupations, however, are suitable for shadowing. One simply needs to find the right situation. Guidance counselors, family, friends, coaches, teammates, and community members can be helpful in identifying an appropriate contact person. It's often easier to set up a shadowing experience with someone you know personally or through a third party (e.g., your guidance counselor or coach). If you're in college, many schools have programs in which graduates have agreed to provide either informational interviews or shadowing opportunities to current students.

The person who agrees to be shadowed is granting you a courtesy. Therefore, it's very important to minimize any inconvenience to that person. Typically, a shadowing experience lasts a couple of hours or up to a half day. Allow your contact person to select a suitable time and date. Confirm your appointment several days before your visit. Arrive just before the arranged time and leave promptly as scheduled. Make sure that your appearance is neat. It's best to ask your contact person about what type of clothing you should wear. Take notes after your visit and send a thank-you note within one day.

During your visit try to picture yourself in the job. Are the tasks interesting to you? Would you like to work in this type of setting? What types of people would you interact with? Would this job reward your values? How would you feel about yourself if you did this job every day? By asking yourself questions like these you'll get a better idea of why this job might be appealing to you.

Internships are a more extended opportunity for acquiring career information. Internships are programs designed for people to learn about occupations through actual work experience. Many high schools and colleges offer course credits for completing an internship. In addition, some communities, especially in major cities, offer paid summer internship programs. Each program differs in requirements and eligibility, so it's best to gather information from local sources. High school guidance counselors and career centers on college campuses usually receive information about federal, state, and local programs. Local libraries may also receive internship information. Obtain this information early because some internship programs require a one-year commitment and you'll need to plan accordingly.

An example of a paid internship is the United States Olympic Committee's Olympic Job Opportunity Program (OJOP). This program allows Olympic-level athletes to gather paid work experience in companies throughout the United States. The companies grant athletes flexible work schedules so they can continue to train for their sport. The company benefits by gaining employees who are achievement oriented. The athletes gain by being paid for work experience that doesn't interfere with their training schedule.

CHAPTER SUMMARY

In this chapter, you've learned about the world of work and how to acquire occupational and career information. The occupations are organized by different fields as well as different levels. Occupational fields typically correspond to the interest areas that you read about and used in the self-exploration chapter. This correspondence helps you to compare your interests, values, and skills to different occupational fields.

You should realize that career exploration continues throughout life. You may repeat this cycle several times before arriving at an initial choice. Even after making an initial choice it's likely that you'll repeat the career exploration process several times in your lifetime. Career exploration skills are valuable assets. Once you learn them, they'll be available whenever you need them.

In this chapter, you should have learned the following:

1. Occupations are typically organized by how they relate to data, people, and things or by the Holland themes.

2. Library resources such as the *Occupational Outlook Handbook* provide a representative overview of many occupational areas.

3. An informational interview is an effective way of gather information about careers.

4. Shadowing and internships provide opportunities to observe and experience actual work practices.

Chapter 7

Career Action Plan

Now that you've learned more about yourself and how to identify careers that are consistent with your personal values, interests, and skills, it's time to put everything together into your career action plan. The key to getting the career that's right for you is having a specific goal and a solid plan to reach it. Hubie Brown, a long-time coach in the National Basketball Association and now a television commentator, is fond of saying, "One of the most common problems in our society is unsuccessful people with great potential." We can all think of many examples of individuals with tremendous talent and skills who never reach their potential. People achieve their fullest potential when they use all of their skills to attain their goals.

As athletes progress along their athletic life cycle they meet other athletes who have equal physical ability. Elite athletes know that physical skills alone aren't enough to ensure continued success in their sport. The higher you go in your sport, the more you'll need to develop your mental skills.

The mental skills you use in your sport can also help you in your job search. The most important of these mental skills is your ability to set and attain goals. A goal is a dream you're willing to work hard to reach. However, even when you're committed and willing to work hard, it may be difficult to attain a goal that isn't designed in a way that enables you to reach it. The purpose of this chapter is to teach you how to identify goals and how to develop a game plan to attain them.

STEP 1: DEFINING GOALS

The first step in setting effective career goals is to define the goals in a manner that will increase the likelihood of success. To do that, each goal must

1. be stated positively,
2. identify specific behaviors, and
3. be under your control.

Let's examine each of these three requirements in more depth. First, when you're unhappy with your performance in sport, you probably tend to focus on the problems you're having. Although identifying problems may help you pinpoint areas you need to work on, this focus places your attention on your mistakes. It's much more effective to focus on what you need to do to improve rather than what you want to avoid. When you try *not* to make a mistake, you end up with a focus on a negative. If you're trying not to miss a free throw or not to be nervous during a job interview, your focus is on a negative behavior. Having a negative focus usually ensures a negative outcome. Try, for example, not to think of chocolate for 30 seconds. Difficult, isn't it? Now, instead of trying not to think of chocolate, concentrate on your best athletic performance ever or your ideal job. Picture it clearly, and remember how it felt or would feel. Get a good picture of it. Now, are you still thinking about chocolate? Focusing on positive goals helps you understand what you want, what new skills you need to learn, and what obstacles you need to overcome to reach these goals.

When the focus is on something you want, rather than on something you wish to avoid, the outcome is more likely to be positive. In identifying positive goals about your career, consider the following: What would have to happen for me to feel good about the process of choosing my career?

What values, interests, and skills do I have that will help me?

Second, you must identify the goal in specific terms. Specific means concrete, observable activities—in other words, something that you can see and measure. Consider as an example the following conversation between two students:

Student A: I'd like to be less uptight before the interview.

Student B: What do you mean by "uptight"? That sounds negative.

Student A: Well then, I'd like to feel more relaxed and less tense when I'm talking to someone about a job opening.

Student B: Specifically, how would you like to feel, or what would you like to do before the interview?

Student A: I'd like to learn how to relax myself and be able to practice that feeling while I'm waiting for the interview to begin.

Setting goals that are both positive and specific is important. Talking it over with someone who can assist you in clarifying your goal while not giving advice may help. Carrying on an imaginary conversation with yourself to clarify the goal may also help.

A third important element in goal setting is to make sure that you have control over the goals that you set. Since you have control only over your own actions, appropriate goals are ones that represent changes in your actions, not the actions of others. Consider the following conversation:

Athlete A: I'd like to have a job lined up before I graduate.

Athlete B: I'm sure most people would like to have a job offer before they graduate, but getting one isn't totally under your control. What specific things could you do to improve your chances of getting one?

Athlete A: Well, if I could get my resume done, get my credentials on file with the College Placement Center, and line up a few references, it would really help my chances, if something came up.

In the preceding situation the athlete has changed the goal to focus on a part of the job-hunting process over which he or she has control. It would be similar to a tennis player setting a goal of winning every tournament for the year. Remember, winning isn't a goal, it's a result. The tennis player could get sick, have an off day, be the victim of some bad calls, or just meet a hot opponent. It would certainly be great if she won every tournament, but she doesn't have complete control over the result. She can, however, control how many serves she practices each day, and she knows that she wins matches when she gets 70 percent of her first serves in. The same is true of getting a job. Securing your perfect job requires more than wanting it; you must be willing to identify specific actions that you're willing to do or improve—these are the goals—and commit yourself to learning how to take these actions at the highest possible level. For example, if your perfect job is to be a sports reporter, you could set a goal to do 10 informational interviews with print and television reporters to develop a better understanding of the field. Or you could set a goal to take a creative writing course and write a minimum of an hour every day.

To help you explore your goal(s), respond to the questions and statements in worksheet 7.1, the Goal Identification Guide.

Worksheet 7.1:
Goal Identification Guide

A. What is your short- or long-term career goal (for example, to write a resume, to develop a career plan, to get into a college degree program)?

B. State your goal in positive terms.

C. Describe your career goal.

1. When did you decide to work toward this goal?

2. What have you already done, if anything, to try to achieve this goal?

3. What thoughts and feelings do you have when you think about this goal?

4. When would you like to achieve this goal?

D. State your goal using specific actions you'll have to take to reach your goal (for example, completing my resume by reading a resume-writing book, filling in a resume worksheet as shown in chapter 9, and having three people evaluate a draft of my resume).

E. If any of the actions you described aren't under your control, such as waiting for the personnel office to review your resume, restate the goal using actions that are under your control.

F. Summary and evaluation.
   1. Is the goal positive?   Yes _____   No _____
   2. Have you identified specific actions to reach the goal?
      Yes _____   No _____
   3. Does the goal relate exclusively to actions under your control?
      Yes _____   No _____
   4. If you checked "no" for any of the three questions, restate the goal to make certain that it is positive, specific, and under your control.

STEP 2: DETERMINING THE IMPORTANCE OF THE GOAL

In the following examples, notice how the individual avoids using statements like " I want to . . ." or "I would like to . . ."

- "My parents want me to choose a major this month."
- "I ought to study harder."
- "My coach wants me to lose weight."

Some goals result from what other people want you to do. For example, unless you can honestly state, "I would like to lose weight" or, "I would like to study harder," it's unlikely that you'll have the commitment necessary to reach the goal. When it comes to personal goals, most people do what they want, not what they're told they ought to or should do. Thus, when you accept a goal that isn't truly your own, you won't likely work as hard to achieve it. This was the case for Claire, a national lacrosse team member, who eventually dropped out of law school even though her mother and older sister were lawyers. Claire explained, "From day one, everybody just figured I would join the firm, but it's not what I wanted to do. Maybe that's why I found it so hard to study. Now that I'm designing clothes, I feel so much more alive." You must be committed to a goal to work effectively toward achieving it. Your goals must also be realistic. Trying to reach impossible goals will be frustrating and disappointing.

Now complete worksheet 7.2, the Goal Importance Guide, using the same goal you identified in worksheet 7.1, the Goal Identification Guide.

Worksheet 7.2:
Goal Importance Guide

Why is this goal important to me in my career plan?

1. To whom is the goal most important?

   _____ Me

   _____ A significant person in my life

   Person's name _____

2. Is the goal something I believe I ought to or should accomplish?

   _____ Feel "ought to" or "should" accomplish

   _____ "Want" to accomplish

3. How will my feelings about myself change if I choose to work toward this career goal?

   How will my feelings about myself change if I choose not to work toward this career goal?

4. How will my relationships with others, such as my family or coach, change if I choose to work toward this career goal?

How will my relationships with others change if I choose not to?

5. Is my career goal based on the following?

_____ Realistic interests, wishes, or expectations?

_____ Overdemanding expectations of others?

_____ Wishful thinking?

_____ Other factors?

6. From my perspective, is it worthwhile for me to try to achieve this goal?   Yes _____   No _____

7. How will attaining this particular career goal affect my life?

8. Do I think I can reach this goal?   Yes _____   No _____

STEP 3: ROADBLOCKS TO ACHIEVING THE GOAL

In this step we'll help you explore what might prevent you from achieving the goal. In other words, this step involves finding out what it would take for you to arrive at the goal. It's important to focus on the present and the future when you're considering what might keep you from reaching your goals. Delving into the past to discover why you can't achieve a goal is unlikely to be helpful. You should consider four kinds of roadblocks:

1. ***Knowledge Roadblocks.*** You lack information needed to reach the goal. For example, a student who wants to find a summer internship may not know where to look; a student who wants to know what history majors do after earning a degree may not know whom to talk to. If you can say, "I need to *know* . . . ," you lack knowledge.

2. ***Skill Roadblocks.*** You lack the ability to reach the goal because you don't have the necessary skills. There are two kinds of skills: physical skills, and mental or life skills. For example, if a gymnast doesn't know how to do a specific routine, she lacks a physical skill; if she doesn't know how to relax or how to imagine herself being successful either as a gymnast or in a job, she lacks a mental skill. As we mentioned earlier, you can transfer many of the mental skills you've learned in sport to other areas of your life. If you can say, "I need to know *how to* . . . ," you lack skill.

3. ***Risk-Taking Roadblocks.*** You know what to do and how to do it (you have the knowledge and skills), but are unable to take the risk involved in reaching for the goal. Risk is defined as the perceived benefit of an action minus the perceived cost. If you feel the perceived benefit outweighs the perceived cost, the risk is one you may take. If you feel the perceived cost outweighs the perceived benefit, you aren't likely to take the risk. For example, a student wants to apply for a summer job but is afraid he won't be successful; a student may want to major in English but fears she won't be able to get a good job after graduation. If you can say, "I know how to but I'm *afraid* to try . . . ," you lack risk-taking ability.

4. ***Social-Support Roadblocks.*** You have the knowledge and skill and are willing to take the risk but feel that important people in your life won't understand or help you reach your goal. For example, a student may want to become a teacher but feels his parents won't approve because they want him to go into the family business; a student may want to study harder but feels her friends will tease her for working hard. Social supports are especially important when trying to maintain new behaviors. If you can say, "I know how to do it and am willing to take the risk but don't feel the support of my friends (coaches, parents) . . . ," you lack social support.

In many situations, some combination of skills, knowledge, risk-taking, and social-support roadblocks are involved. Some questions that will help you identify roadblocks are the following:

1. What new ways of acting or new skills would you have to acquire to achieve the goal? (skills)
2. What do you need to know to achieve the goal? (knowledge)
3. Since you know what to do to get to your goal, what makes it hard for you to take the chance? (risk)
4. Whom would you talk to about your goal? Whose reactions and help do you need? (support)

Because roadblocks often block the path to your goal, you should have a strategy to handle them. Let's begin by examining some of the roadblocks that may get in the way of the goal you selected in the Goal Identification Worksheet. Complete worksheet 7.3, the Goal Roadblock Guide.

Worksheet 7.3:

Goal Roadblock Guide

What is your understanding of why you haven't achieved the goal?

1. Knowledge roadblock

   Describe _____

   _____

   _____

   _____

2. Skill roadblock

   Describe _____

   _____

   _____

   _____

3. Risk-taking roadblock

   Describe _____

   _____

   _____

   _____

4. Social support roadblock

   Describe _____

   _____

   _____

   _____

5. Some combination of knowledge, skills, risk-taking, and social support roadblocks

   Describe _____

   _____

   _____

   _____

STEP 4: OVERCOMING ROADBLOCKS

Once you've identified a workable goal, the process of trying to reach it, called goal attainment, can begin. Although setting goals and attaining goals are two separate steps, they are interdependent. When you set goals that are negative, vaguely stated, or dependent on someone else's behavior, reaching the goal becomes difficult, if not impossible. Thus, while the process of goal setting influences whether you can reach the goal, the real work occurs after you set the goal—during the goal attainment process. As Vonnie Gros, 1980 and 1984 U.S. Olympic field hockey coach has stated, "The will to succeed is the single-minded desire to conquer the obstacles between where you are now and where you would like to be." For goal attainment, think of "obstacles" as roadblocks, and "single-minded desire" as the energy required to achieve the goal.

In worksheet 7.3, you identified some possible roadblocks to achieving your goal. The process of overcoming these roadblocks is critical to reaching your goal.

The first step to goal attainment is choosing a strategy. Whatever the strategy, you must plan it well. The process of planning directs the energy necessary to overcome specific roadblocks. Effort and hard work aren't sufficient. It's similar to the often quoted business concept "Work smarter, not harder."

We've developed worksheet 7.4, Overcoming Roadblocks, to help you plan your strategy to overcome your roadblocks. Remember the following points:

- To develop skill, you must develop a step-by-step process (see worksheet 7.5).

- To develop knowledge, you can use two types and sources of information—formal and informal. Examples of formal sources are books, newspapers, and classes. Informal sources may be the experience or advice of friends, family, team members, and coworkers. Identify both formal and informal sources that you can and will contact.

- To develop risk-taking ability, consider ways to increase perceived benefits or decrease perceived costs.

- For support, consider what kind of support you need, from whom it is likely to come, and how to ask for it.

Remember, if the goal is important to you, the roadblock is most likely not a lack of motivation. A lack of skills or fear of taking a risk is often disguised as a lack of motivation.

Worksheet 7.4:
Overcoming Roadblocks

A. What is your goal?

_____

_____

B. Could you achieve the goal by knowledge alone?

1. _____ No; if no, go on to "C."

2. _____ Yes; if yes, what knowledge would be necessary?

_____

_____

3. How might you plan to get the information you need? (Consider what information is necessary and both formal and informal sources of information.)

_____

_____

_____

_____

_____

_____

C. Could you achieve the goal if you were more willing to take a risk?

1. _____ No; if no, go on to "D."

2. _____ Yes; if yes, describe the risks you have to take.

_____

_____

3. What are the perceived benefits of seeking the goal?

_____

_____

4. What are the perceived costs of seeking the goal?

_____

_____

5. How might the perceived benefits be increased or the perceived costs decreased so that action is more likely?

_____

D. Could you achieve the goal if you had the support of others?
  1. _____ No; if no, go on to "E."
  2. _____ Yes; if yes, describe the kind of support you need.

_____
_____
_____

  3. From whom is this support needed?

_____
_____
_____

  4. How can I ask for the support?

_____
_____
_____

E. If you've answered "no" to all roadblocks, go back to the goal to see if it is stated correctly, or seek advice on what else could be preventing you from reaching your goal.

STEP 5: DEVELOPING AN ACTION PLAN

Consider the words of John Nabor, 1976 Olympian and winner of seven gold medals.

> In 1972, Mark Spitz won seven gold medals, breaking seven world records. I was at home watching him on my living-room floor. And I said to myself at that time, "Wouldn't it be nice to be able to win a gold medal, to be able to be a world champion in Olympic competition." So right then I had this dream of being an Olympic champion. But right about then it became a goal. That dream-to-goal transition is the biggest thing I learned prior to Olympic competition—how important it is to set a goal. Certainly, motivation is important. A lot of kids have motivation. "Gee, I'd love to be great."

My personal best in the 100 back was 59.5. Roland Matthes, winning the same event for the second consecutive Olympics (1972), went 56.3. I extrapolated his, you know, three Olympic performances and I figured in 1976, 55.5 would have been the order of the day. That's what I figured I would have to do. So I'm four seconds off in the shortest backstroke event on the Olympic program. It's the equivalent of dropping four seconds in the 440-yard dash. It's a substantial chunk. But because it's a goal, now I can decisively figure out how I can attack it. I have four years to do it. I'm watching TV in 1972. I've got four years to train. So it's only one second a year. That's still a substantial chunk. Swimmers train 10 or 11 months a year so it's about a tenth of a second a month, giving time off for missed workouts. And you figure we train six days a week so it's only 1/300th of a second a day. We train from 6:00 to 8:00 in the morning and 4:00 to 6:00 at night, so it's really only about 1/1,200th of a second every hour. Do you know how short a 1,200th of a second is? Look at my hand and blink when I snap. Would you please? OK, from the time your eyelids started to close to the time they touched, 5/1,200ths of a second elapsed. For me to stand on a pool deck and say, "During the next 60 minutes I'm going to improve that much," that's a believable dream. I can believe in myself. I can't believe that I'm going to drop four seconds by the next Olympics. But I can believe I can get that much faster. Couldn't you? Sure! So all of sudden I'm moving.

As you read in the above example, if you have a well-developed plan, you'll probably be more successful in reaching your goals. In developing your goal action plan, you'll need to break your goal down into smaller steps. If John Nabor had tried to take four seconds off his fastest time in the 100-meter backstroke in one step, he might have become frustrated and discouraged. By breaking his goal down into smaller steps, he was able to increase the possibility of attaining his goal. The same will be true for you.

A second benefit of breaking your goal down into smaller steps is that this approach will give you a starting point. There is an old proverb that says "The longest journey starts with a single step." The same is true for your goal-setting strategy. You need to know what to do first to prepare the way for the other steps.

We've found that the best way to prepare your goal action plan is to think of goal attainment as climbing a ladder. If you take it one step at a

Sample Goal Ladder

Goal: I would like to apply for a summer internship in my field.

Step 10. Follow up any interviews, either in person or on the phone, with a thank-you letter.
Due date: _5/30_   Outcome: _____

Step 9. Have a mock interview both in person and on the phone. Rehearse questions that employer might ask me.
Due date: _5/20_   Outcome: _____

Step 8. Send application and ask faculty to send letters.
Due date: _5/15_   Outcome: _____

Step 7. Complete applications with cover letter highlighting my strengths. Ask someone I respect to read it and give me comments.
Due date: _4/30_   Outcome: _____

Step 6. Ask three faculty I know and who respect me to write recommendation letters.
Due date: _4/20_   Outcome: _____

Step 5. Write away for information and applications to the businesses I identified.
Due date: _4/15_   Outcome: _____

Step 4. Prepare a resume and identify skills that will be valuable to the organizations to which I am applying.
Due date: _4/7_   Outcome: _____

Step 3. Identify approximately 10 businesses that offer summer internships that interest me.
Due date: _3/29_   Outcome: _____

Step 2. Go to the Career Center and library to seek information about summer internships in my field.
Due date: _3/20_   Outcome: _____

Step 1. Develop a plan (goal ladder) to reach my goal.
Due date: _3/18_   Outcome: _completed_

time, you'll usually reach the top. We call this strategy a goal ladder. Highlight box 7.1 on page 152 shows you what a goal ladder might look like for someone who wants a summer internship. As you read the sample goal ladder, start reading at step 1, the bottom rung of the ladder.

To develop a goal ladder, you should list all the things that you should do to reach your goal. Next you need to look at your list and put them in order from the ones that you need to do first to those that you should do as you're closer to achieving your goal. By doing this you're building the steps on your ladder, just as we did in building the 10-step ladder in the summer internship example

Examine the practice goal ladder in worksheet 7.5 on page 156. Note that for each rung on the ladder, we've included a space for you to record your due date and outcome. Having deadlines helps you reach your long-term goals on time, and recording outcomes helps you see that you're making progress. Remember, each step should be positive, specific, and under your control.

Now select a goal and complete worksheet 7.5, Your Goal Ladder. Remember that the first steps should be relatively easy to accomplish.

Review each of the steps on your goal ladder. Are there any roadblocks that could prevent you from accomplishing any of the steps? If yes, complete worksheets 7.6 on page 157 so you can plan your strategy to deal with the roadblock.

Now you've learned how to develop your career action plan. No matter where you are in the career development process, you can use the action plan to develop a goal ladder to help you reach your goals. This goal-setting model can help you not only in your career planning but also in your sport and personal life. If you don't set goals, you're like a computer without a program. Following the steps in goal setting will put you on the fast track for success.

CHAPTER SUMMARY

In this chapter, you've learned to develop your career action plan by using a goal-setting strategy. You may have already used goal setting to help you improve your sport skills. Now you know how to transfer that skill to the career search process. In the next three chapters, we'll teach you some of the specific tools necessary to get a job. Using your new goal-setting skills will enable you to master these tools quickly and set you up for a successful job-hunting campaign.

Worksheet 7.5:

Your Goal Ladder

Your goal: _____

Step 10: Due date: Outcome:
Step 9: Due date: Outcome:
Step 8: Due date: Outcome:
Step 7: Due date: Outcome:
Step 6: Due date: Outcome:
Step 5: Due date: Outcome:
Step 4: Due date: Outcome:
Step 3: Due date: Outcome:
Step 2: Due date: Outcome:
Step 1: Due date: Outcome:

Worksheet 7.6:
Possible Roadblocks to Goal Attainment

Roadblocks	*Ways to overcome roadblocks*
Step 10: a. _____ b. _____	
Step 9: a. _____ b. _____	
Step 8: a. _____ b. _____	
Step 7: a. _____ b. _____	
Step 6: a. _____ b. _____	
Step 5: a. _____ b. _____	
Step 4: a. _____ b. _____	
Step 3: a. _____ b. _____	
Step 2: a. _____ b. _____	
Step 1: a. _____ b. _____	

From this chapter, you should have learned the following:

1. Goals should be positively stated, specific, and under your control.
2. You are much more likely to reach a goal that *you* want to achieve, rather than a goal that someone else believes you should reach.
3. There are often roadblocks that get in the way of goal attainment. The most common roadblocks are a lack of knowledge, a lack of skill, fear of taking risks, and a lack of social support.
4. You can use several strategies to overcome roadblocks to goal attainment.
5. The key to a well-developed career action plan is a goal ladder.
6. Goal ladders break goals down into manageable steps and give you a clear starting point.
7. Roadblocks can occur at any point on the way up a goal ladder. When roadblocks occur, the strategies that you learned to cope with them should become new parts of your goal ladder.

PART III

Career Acquisition

Chapter
8

The Career Search

Now that you've learned a little more about yourself and the various careers available to you, it's time to look at specific tools and job-hunting strategies that can help you get the job that's right for you. Before we begin, however, it's important to explore some of the myths and realities of job hunting.

TODAY'S JOB MARKET

If you were to scan the headlines of the business pages of any major newspaper, you might wonder about your chances of getting a job. Readers are bombarded every day with negative economic forecasts and announcements of major corporate layoffs. The truth is that people are still finding jobs. Employment is shifting away from large corporations toward smaller emerging companies. This shift seems to be fueled by several recent corporate trends.

The first is downsizing. Today's corporations seem to be adopting the old Arkansas football strategy of being lean and mean. To become more efficient and productive, many corporations have turned to technology and innovation. As a result, companies need many fewer workers to perform required tasks.

The second trend is mergers and takeovers. In today's economy, many corporations are buying out their competition or merging with similar businesses. When this happens corporations often have two people performing the same function, and they are able to eliminate one of the positions.

The third trend is outsourcing. Corporations have discovered that it costs less to have outside companies perform some of the tasks that their employees once performed. For example, it may be more cost effective for corporations to hire small, specialized companies to manage functions such as payroll, computer servicing, or legal counsel than to employ their own specialists. This trend saves money on benefits and overhead while ensuring specialized services.

As these trends shrink the corporate workforce, a major upswing has occurred in the number of new companies and consulting firms in the technology and service industries. These smaller companies or firms are expanding rapidly and will continue to offer a large number of varied employment opportunities. This fact becomes particularly important because most career counselors believe that as many as 85 percent of jobs are never listed in newspapers or professional publications. Many of the jobs that make up this so-called hidden job market are in smaller companies that may have much different hiring policies than large corporations. While we've focused on the corporate sector to this point, the same trends are occurring in other professional environments as well. Nonprofit organizations such as colleges, public schools, civil service agencies, and health care organizations have also responded to a changing world. Many of these organizations have followed the corporate lead by downsizing and outsourcing. If you have a special interest in occupations like coaching, teaching, or providing health care services, you may find it necessary to take a creative approach to the job search to obtain a position.

Some fields will have more positions available than others. What are some of the jobs that might provide the greatest opportunity in the next 10 years? Well, according to *Money* magazine, which recently rated America's 50 hottest jobs, the top 10 jobs in the next decade will be computer engineer, computer system analyst, physical therapist, special education teacher, private investigator, radiological technician, legal assistant, preschool and kindergarten teacher, entertainer, and legal/medical secretary. If you happen to be interested in a sports-related career, sports instructors and coaches at the high school level were ranked 29th.

If you're concerned about your chances of getting a job in a certain field or want to see which professional areas have the most opportunities, you may find it helpful to look at reports printed annually by a number of organizations. The *Occupational Outlook Handbook,* published by the U.S. Department of Labor, is the most popular of these publications. This report, available at most public libraries, provides a wealth of information about the future job market. For example, a recent edition predicted that the greatest number of new jobs will be in the service industry. These jobs all involve some form of service to others in business, health care, and social service settings. The *American Almanac of Jobs and Salaries* is also a useful tool when you're trying to find out about the changing job market. The reference librarian at your local library can assist you with these and other sources of information.

Even after selecting a career path that seems to have good prospects for employment, you'll find that getting a job in today's economy requires much skill and direct action. People who rely on the traditional job-hunting method of reading the help wanted ads and sending out resumes to every job that is close to their area of training and experience often encounter little success and many rejections. Today you need to know what you want to do, have a specific game plan to get it, and work hard to give yourself the best chances to get the right job. Remember, you should consider getting a job a job in itself. As such, you need to spend ample time, energy, and resources to be successful. In the next sections, we'll give you some strategies to help you target career possibilities.

THE JOB SEARCH

In general, you should approach your job search the way you would prepare for a big game or competition. You need to do three things:

1. Scout the opposition, the arena, and the event setting.
2. Get your team ready.
3. Get yourself ready.

The same is true for the job search. Instead of scouting your opponent, you need to discover what's out there. In the job search you'll get your team ready by using your support team, and you'll get yourself ready by preparing for your job search. In this chapter, we'll help you organize your job search scouting report and your support team. In chapters 9 and 10, we'll help you develop the skills and tools that you'll need to prepare yourself to get a job.

Scouting Report

Although developing scouting reports on potential employers is similar to developing reports for athletic opponents, there is one big difference. In sport you typically know whom you're going to play. This isn't true of the job hunt, where your first task is to identify companies or organizations that may be able to hire you. Imagine what it would be like if you had to develop a scouting report on all 64 teams that will play in the NCAA men's basketball tournament this year. Most people would find that an impossible task. Fortunately, NCAA tourney teams play in brackets that limit the number of possible opponents and make the preparation task more manageable.

To facilitate your search, you need to create a job search bracket, targeting specific companies or organizations within a specific location. Therefore, your first task is to decide where you would like to work. Some people are wide open to any possibility and are willing to relocate to any part of the world to land the right job, but most have preferences that would narrow their choices to specific locations. By answering the questions in worksheet 8.1 you'll examine some of the considerations that will be part of this decision.

Now that you have a better idea of the location where you would like to work, your next task is to identify specific companies or organizations within that location that might be able to offer you interesting employment within your career area. You can use several strategies to identify potential employers within your target area.

1. Read through local newspaper want ads, trade publications, professional journals, and business periodicals. Carefully reading want ads may help you identify possible jobs that you may not have considered just by the job title. Remember, you're trying to find positions that match your interests, skills, and needs. You may not be familiar with the job title, but you may have the skills and interest to do the job. Take the time to examine the specific words that the employer uses to describe a position. Action words, such as lead, analyze, or motivate, may match the transferable skills you identified in chapter 5 and lead you to new job possibilities.

Worksheet 8.1:

Location Rating Scorecard

This scorecard will help you determine your most important considerations when deciding where you would like to live.

Part 1: Rate each item according to its importance to you. Use the following scale.

Very important = 3   Moderately important = 2   Not important = 1

Rating	*Selection criteria*
1. _____	Proximity to family and friends
2. _____	Cost of living
3. _____	Affordability of housing
4. _____	Access to sport and recreational opportunities
5. _____	Weather and climate
6. _____	Cultural and religious opportunities
7. _____	Ease of transportation
8. _____	Educational opportunities for self and family
9. _____	Access to major metropolitan areas
10. _____	Job availability

Part 2: Build your location rating scorecard by listing the most important items from part 1 and adding other items that are critical to your selection of an appropriate location. For example, if you're still training, you may be locked into a specific location to have access to facilities or coaching.

After you build your personalized scorecard, use it to rate locations that you're considering. If you have several items that have to be met (e.g., proximity to family or coaches), you can quickly narrow down your possibilities by eliminating all locations that don't meet your critical needs.

Location _____

Rating	*Selection criteria*
1. _____	_____
2. _____	_____
3. _____	_____
4. _____	_____
5. _____	_____
6. _____	_____
7. _____	_____
8. _____	_____
9. _____	_____
10. _____	_____
_____	**Total**

2. Look for possible leads in job ads or newspaper columns for jobs that an employer hasn't yet advertised. Company expansions and new product lines may be signs of new job possibilities. If Company X announces that they are expanding into the personal computer market, it could mean that they will need additional sales, marketing, or technical people. By contacting Company X directly and exploring job possibilities, you may beat other candidates to the punch and land a job within your selected field.

3. Be careful not to fall for dead-end ads such as blind ads that don't give company names or ads that hint that you'll have to make an investment before the company hires you. Ads that have you reply to a mail box number without identifying the company or ads that claim huge financial gains for minimum effort on your part are usually a waste of your time. Such ads are frustrating because you rarely get a reply from the company and you have no way of following up on the lead.

4. Avoid using position-wanted ads to advertise yourself. They are usually not an effective way of getting a job and often lead you to become targets of placement agencies that charge substantial fees for their services.

5. Find new and different newspapers, journals, and association newsletters in your public library or a local college library. Librarians can be extremely helpful in directing you to chamber of commerce listings, books related to your field, out-of-town phone directories, and newspapers from other areas.

6. Watch for people on the move. When people take new jobs, their old positions usually become available. Speaking to people about their old positions can sometimes get you a head start over other applicants.

7. Use state employment agencies and college placement centers to find job listings that may not be published in newspapers and periodicals. If you're currently enrolled or an alumnus of a college or university, you're probably eligible for all their placement services, including job listings, job credential services, and computer and on-line placement assistance.

8. Get on-line. You can use computer interest groups to get information about potential locations and identify local contacts that can facilitate your search. Many interest groups also list job openings and identify people who have taken new jobs. However, be very cautious before using any electronic job bank service that requires hefty user fees.

Following these suggestions will help you identify potential employers within your target area. Before we show you how to develop scouting reports to evaluate whether the companies that you identified will meet your career development needs, we need to consider how your support system can assist in the career search process.

Using Your Support Team to Help in the Job Search

There is an old adage that says "It's who you know" that is important in getting a job. Although that may not seem fair, positions in today's job market often go to people whom the employer knows directly or indirectly. The trick is to meet as many people as you can in your desired field. You may have already begun to make some job contacts while doing informational interviewing as part of your career exploration. Now you need to continue to expand upon this contact network by targeting people in your desired field.

As an athlete, you've already met many people who can help you in the job search, perhaps by finding hidden jobs or in putting you in touch with people who may be able to create a job specifically for you. The trick is knowing how to organize your search and how to use these people effectively.

One athlete who participated in the U.S. Olympic Committee's CAPA Program was able to use her athletic status to develop a broad range of contacts. Her case clearly illustrates a number of strategies to build a systematic network of potential job contacts.

Rochelle's Story

Rochelle was the daughter of middle-class parents who encouraged her natural interest in athletics. The family lived in a suburb of Los Angeles. Blessed with great speed and excellent hand-eye coordination, Rochelle excelled at a variety of sports, but her height led her to concentrate her energies on her favorite sport, basketball. By age 16 she had played competitive softball, basketball, volleyball, tennis, and soccer and had tried out sports such as surfing, golf, cycling, and swimming. In her junior year at high school, she was selected to attend a national developmental camp, where her natural abilities brought her to the attention of several collegiate coaches. Rochelle was heavily recruited out of high school and eventually chose to attend a major southeastern university known for its excellence in both academics and athletics.

In her freshman year Rochelle played so well that she won a spot on a national development team that toured Australia and New Zealand that summer. She played a lot of basketball and made many contacts in the Australian and New Zealand basketball communities. In her sophomore year Rochelle won the starting power forward spot. She started every game over the next three seasons. At the same time, she maintained a 3.8 average in her classes and was frequently on the dean's list. In the break between her junior and senior years, Rochelle used her university's cooperative education program to land an internship with a local computer-consulting firm. She graduated as a business major with a specialty in computers.

From the time she entered college, Rochelle impressed coaches and advisors with her aggressive approach to career development. As she traveled around the country on competition trips, Rochelle handed out her personal card to many people she met, including sponsors, supporters, and sports officials. The card, provided to all the members of the team, stated simply "Rochelle ———, women's basketball team." Rochelle collected hundreds of business cards from these contacts and stored them alphabetically in a plastic folder. Those who met her at after-game dinners or sponsor-related functions remember that she was never afraid to ask questions and that she showed great interest in the careers of those she met, often questioning them at length about the type of work they did and how they got started in their business.

In the spring of her senior year, Rochelle traveled to the Olympic Training Center in Colorado Springs to try out for the USA women's basketball team. After four days of exhausting workouts and training sessions, Rochelle won a spot on the Olympic team, one of just 12 athletes to make the squad. The team excelled at the games and won the gold medal, after a stirring semifinal victory that saw them rally from 5 points down with six minutes to play. Rochelle averaged 12 points and 11 rebounds per game, and the coach was full of praise for her play.

After taking two months off after the Olympics, Rochelle had conversations with several schools who recruited her to be an assistant coach, but she eventually decided to end her career in basketball. Rochelle believed that she had reached the level of excellence she had aimed at in the sport and that her Olympic experience had been a tremendous bonus for her. The job market was tight when Rochelle finished her degree, but she landed a good job with the second company with which she had interviewed. A deciding factor in her final interview was her response to a question posed to all three final candidates for the position. Minutes before a meeting with the selection panel for the job, Rochelle was given a blank piece of paper and asked to fill up the sheet by writing down as much about herself as she could. After completing sections about her education, job experience, and career goals, Rochelle still had two inches of blank space at the bottom of the page. After being stuck for a moment, she wrote down the name of every state and country she had visited during her extensive basketball tours. When she sat down to meet the panel, the first questions they asked were about the exotic locales she had mentioned on her interview sheet.

After six productive years with that firm, Rochelle, now married, left to start a consulting business with a colleague in Los Angeles. After a rough start-up year they experienced considerable success. Rochelle displayed many of the work skills that she had shown in basketball years before. She was proud of her basketball career, and at the bottom of her business card was a line that read "Member of the USA gold medal women's basketball team, —— Olympic Games." Rochelle had kept in touch with many of the people she had

> *met while playing basketball. As she and her partner expanded their business, these contacts proved to be valuable sources of information about business opportunities. Rochelle became an active, well-known member of her community, and after the birth of her first child she became head of the local chamber of commerce. She was the first black woman to gain that distinction. When young people ask her for advice on how to get started in a career, she tells them this: "Pay attention to all the great lessons you learn in sport. My sporting career helped me a great deal, and it can help you, too, if you keep your eyes and ears open."*

As you read Rochelle's story, you may have noticed that she started making contacts long before she decided to retire from competitive basketball. By age 16, Rochelle had already made many contacts that played an important role in her career search. By making these contacts, Rochelle was using an important skill called networking.

Networking

A network is a group of people who know that you're looking for a job. These people know what skills you have and what careers you're exploring. Networking is not the same as informational interviewing, which you learned about in chapter 6, but the two use many of the same techniques. In an informational interview, you're simply asking for information about a job or career. Networking implies that you're actively looking for job openings. Many career counselors believe that the speed with which you find a job is directly related to the number of people in your career network.

Your career network would include

1. your family and their friends;
2. your friends and their families;
3. contacts you've made through sport, school, church, and social activities; and
4. people that you meet through your informational interviews.

As shown in Rochelle's story, you should keep track of the people in your network. We've found that keeping a record of contacts often comes in handy when you're trying to locate specific information. Worksheet 8.2 shows a sample contact card.

Worksheet 8.2:

Your Contact Network

Develop index cards for each person in your career network. Your index card should contain this information:

Contact's name _____

Address _____

_____

_____

Company/organization _____

Telephone number(s) _____

Date of contact _____

Date of follow-up thank-you letter _____

Topics discussed _____

_____

_____

_____

_____

Here are some additional tips to help you expand your contact network.

1. Let many people know that you're looking for a certain type of job. Explain what you would like to do and what skills you have rather than just giving a job title. By doing that, your support people can help you identify additional job titles that may fit your skills.

2. Let all the members of your support team know that you're beginning a job search. This includes family, coaches, teammates, friends, teachers, and other support people you identified in your personal support team.

3. Get involved. By being active in community, social, recreational, and school activities, you can expand your support system and your contact network.

4. Use your athletic experience to promote yourself by accepting speaking engagements with local groups or assisting with sports events in your community.

5. Use college career development and placement services. Many colleges keep a list of alumni who have agreed to assist current students in their job search by sharing information about their careers. You may have already used this list for informational interviews. Using this list to identify contacts in your desired target area can save you much time and greatly expand your network.

PUTTING IT TOGETHER

Now that you've learned how to identify where you would like to work, it's important to organize your career search in a systematic way. Besides maintaining your networking file, it's important to record what you learned about each company or organization that you investigated. Highlight box 8.1 provides a sample position scouting report that shows you how you might record company information. Use worksheet 8.3 to construct a personalized scouting report by deleting unimportant items and adding other items that would be important to finding a good match for your career aspirations.

Congratulations! You now know how to target specific job leads. But you still need to prepare yourself to take advantage of any job opportunities that you might discover. The next two chapters focus on that preparation.

CHAPTER SUMMARY

The ability to identify possible career leads through active research and networking is a critical skill in the job-hunting game. Just as you've learned the skills of your sport, you need to upgrade your skills constantly in this new type of competition. The positive attitudes you learned through sport participation can be the most helpful tool you use as you search for a job. Your past success as an athlete should be a great motivator for being a success in the job market.

Highlight Box 8.1

Sample Position Scouting Report

Rate each item according to its importance to you. Use the following scale.

1	2	3	4	5
Not Important		Moderately Important		Extremely Important

Position: Assistant Manager of Regional Sales

Company: American Sporting Goods

	Rating	*Position criteria*
1.	_____	Location
2.	_____	Salary range
3.	_____	Health and dental plan
4.	_____	Vacation policy
5.	_____	Work hours
6.	_____	Work setting
7.	_____	Travel opportunities
8.	_____	Opportunities for advancement
9.	_____	Employee education and development program
10.	_____	College tuition program
11.	_____	Retirement plan
12.	_____	Job security
13.	_____	Compatibility with coworkers
14.	_____	Flexible work environment
15.	_____	Quality of supervision
16.	_____	Company reputation
17.	_____	Level of authority
18.	_____	Employee morale or spirit
19.	_____	Achievement oriented
20.	_____	Values initiative
21.	_____	Opportunities to use my skills
	_____	*Total*

Worksheet 8.3:

Your Position Scouting Report

Use this form to build your personalized position scouting report. Examine the examples of job criteria shown in the sample position scouting report (highlight box 8.1). Select any items that would be important for your job satisfaction and list them under position characteristics. You can personalize your scouting report further by adding items that are important to you. Remember, a position should match your most important values, interests, and skills.

Rate each item according to its importance to you. Use the following scale.

1	2	3	4	5
Not Important		Moderately Important		Extremely Important

Position: _____

Company: _____

Rating	*Position criteria*
1. _____	Location
2. _____	Salary range
3. _____	Health and dental plan
4. _____	Vacation policy
5. _____	Work hours
6. _____	Work setting
7. _____	Travel opportunities
8. _____	Opportunities for advancement
9. _____	Employee education and development program
10. _____	College tuition program
11. _____	Retirement plan
12. _____	Job security
13. _____	Compatibility with coworkers

14. _____ Flexible work environment _____

15. _____ Quality of supervision _____

16. _____ Company reputation _____

17. _____ Level of authority _____

18. _____ Employee morale or spirit _____

19. _____ Achievement-oriented _____

20. _____ Values initiative _____

21. _____ Opportunities to use my skills _____

In this chapter, we've outlined how to generate and search out job leads and how to get your support team involved in your career search. If you use your goal-setting skills to search actively for job leads, you'll have a much greater chance of landing a position that's right for you. Remember the old adage we shared in the introduction, "Luck is when preparation meets opportunity." If you actively use the skills that you've learned in this chapter, you'll most likely discover job opportunities. In the next two chapters, we help you become prepared to take advantage of those opportunities and get the job that's right for you.

In this chapter, you should have learned the following:

1. Many jobs exist in a hidden job market that requires a more active approach to the job search process.
2. Finding job openings is a job in itself and requires considerable effort.
3. You can employ a number of strategies to find job leads.
4. Networking is a critical skill in the job search process.

Chapter 9

Writing Effective Resumes and Cover Letters

If you've already been out job hunting, you may have discovered that most employers require you to submit a resume and a cover letter. Your resume is a written summary of your skills, talents, and experience. It's your opportunity to make a good impression and show potential employers how your values, interests, and skills match the duties and responsibilities of the job opening they are seeking to fill.

The purpose of the resume and cover letter is to get you a job interview. In just one or two pages, you need to present your qualifications in a manner that convinces employers that you have the skills and attitudes necessary to make a solid contribution to their organization. If you've presented yourself well on paper and match an employer's needs, they'll call you in for an interview. During the interview process you'll have an opportunity to explore how well the position meets your core job requirements. You'll also have an opportunity to convince the hiring person that you can add value to his or her organization. In this chapter, we'll show you how to develop and write effective resumes and cover letters. In the next chapter, we'll get you ready for the job interview.

PREPARING THE RESUME

You may have already had to develop a player profile for a newspaper article, press release, or team yearbook. A resume is quite similar. It lists your "stats" and personal and professional accomplishments that relate to a specific job for which you are applying. However, you need to present that information in a manner that would say to a potential employer, "If you hire me, I'll add value (e.g., money, quality, prestige, problem-solving ability) to your company or organization."

Generally, resumes are one or two pages long and are professionally printed on high-quality paper. They typically include identifying information (e.g., your name, work and home addresses, telephone numbers), your experience or work history, your educational background, any significant awards that you've received, and other information that shows how your experience matches the requirements of a specific job opening. The three common types of resumes are the chronological resume, the functional resume, and the targeted resume. In the sections that follow, we'll show you how to develop resumes of each type so that you can decide which one is best for you. However, we need to begin with some resume-writing basics.

General Resume Guidelines

As you begin to pull together information for your resume, you should know that employers will judge it by both its content and its appearance. If your resume doesn't look good, it probably won't be read. Real estate agents often talk about curb appeal. If a house or property doesn't look well maintained on the outside, it's extremely difficult to get potential buyers to look at the inside. The same is true of your resume. If your resume is cluttered, sloppy, or visually unappealing, it will probably be passed over.

Resume Format

To ensure that your resume has good curb appeal, conform to standard guidelines for format.

1. Use high-quality, 8 1/2-by-11-inch paper.

2. Maintain margins of at least 1 inch.

3. Experiment with the appearance of headings by using capitals, underlining, and bolding to enhance readability. Headings should be consistent throughout the document. Don't use all capitals for one heading and lower case for a similar heading.

4. Use elite, pica, or similar type size and carefully proofread to ensure that the document is free of errors.

5. Organize headings and facts so that the most important information can be seen easily.

6. Use high-quality copy services and high-quality paper.

7. Try to limit your resume to one page, but use two pages rather than cram too much information on one page.

8. Remember that curb appeal is critical. Have several people review your resume to make sure it looks good before you make copies.

If you do a good job of presenting your information, you'll pass the curb appeal test. Now it's time to check out what is inside your resume—the content.

Tips on Resume Content

As you begin to organize the information that you want to display in your resume, consider some of the following resume-writing suggestions:

1. The information should be related to the job for which you are applying. The more you know about the organization or company, the easier it will be for you to match your strengths to their needs.

2. Sentences and paragraphs should be brief but should clearly convey the information that you want to get across.

3. Emphasize specific information that highlights your skills. Using facts and numbers can strengthen the impact of your information.

4. Identify skills and experience in your sport history that could be valuable to the employer in the particular position for which you are applying.

5. Be truthful and use facts to emphasize your accomplishments. Don't sell yourself short.

6. Use verbs that stress the importance of the skills you've learned in and out of sport. Some of these words are listed below:
   - advanced, designed, identified
   - analyzed, demonstrated, implemented
   - coordinated, established, improved
   - created, evaluated, managed
   - compiled, expanded, motivated
   - developed, instructed, negotiated
   - directed, implemented, organized
   - distributed, initiated, supervised

7. Proofread your resume. Have someone who knows about resume writing review it with you. Ask them to make suggestions before you complete your final draft. Remember, if they aren't clear about some of your content, then chances are a potential employer will have the same problem.

8. Ask someone in your network to evaluate your resume to see if it presents the best picture of you and your skills.

Now that you've learned how to improve the appearance and content of your resume, it's time to decide what type or types of resumes will work best for you.

Chronological Resume

If you have a good work history and some recent experience that fits well with the job you are applying for, then the chronological resume may work best. The chronological resume is the most commonly used resume. It lists your job-related experience by date with your most recent experience listed first. Chronological resumes are the easiest to prepare because your work history provides the outline for the content areas. Examine the sample chronological resume in highlight box 9.1.

To help you decide if this type of resume is best for you, complete worksheet 9.1. The information that you provide will form the basic outline for your chronological resume. It's usually helpful if you have a particular job in mind as you fill in your responses.

Functional Resume

School, training, and competition schedules prevent many athletes from establishing consistent work histories. These athletes may have taken

Highlight Box 9.1

Sample Chronological Resume

MARGARET MANNING

Bonatello College, Box 488, Friar, ME 06884

207-555-3621

EDUCATION: **Master of Physical Education, Sports Management,** August 1994

Bonatello College, Friar, ME

Bachelor of Science, Business Administration, May 1993

Eastern Maine State University, Swansea, ME

- Concentration in Management and Marketing
- GPA 3.47/4.0, Dean's List
- Outstanding Scholar Athlete Award (junior and senior years)

SUMMARY OF EXPERIENCE

1993 - Present   **Maine Brewers**, Brunswick, ME

Assistant to the Director, Public Relations Office

- Assist with community and media relations
- Responsible for providing pregame information to the press and professional scouts
- Disseminate game scores and statistics to the media

1992 - 1993   **Bonatello College**, Friar, ME

Student Assistant, Sports Information Office

- Contacted and forwarded to media athletic game scores, statistics, and summaries
- Input athletic statistics into Macintosh computer system database

Spring 1992   **Eastern Maine State University**, Swansea, ME

Internship, Sports Information Director

- Produced the 1992 NEISCA Schedule Book and Directory
- Contacted NEISCA members through distribution of letters and a questionnaire
- Processed and input questionnaire data and schedules into Macintosh system

1989 - 1992   **Eastern Maine State University**, Swansea, ME
Contest Management Assistant/Office Assistant, Athletic Department
- Coordinated game management, including contact with officials, coaches, and team
- Operated clock and scoreboard for volleyball, soccer, basketball, and baseball
- Assisted in preparation of intercollegiate athletic events and special programs: public relations, ticket sales, court and field preparations
- Trained and supervised new student workers on procedures and policies
- Processed computer information: typing, filing, phone operations, photocopying, sorting information

ATHLETIC EXPERIENCE
- Four years EMSU Varsity Soccer Team, Captain, 1991-1992
- 1992 NCAA Women of the Year Award
- Second-Place Team, 1990 NCAA Division III Women's Soccer Tournament
- National Championship Team, 1989 NCAA Division III Soccer Tournament

VOLUNTEER EXPERIENCE
Reading and Drug Literacy Program, Swansea, ME
- Worked with third- and fourth-grade students about staying in school and away from drugs and alcohol

jobs that didn't specifically relate to their career goals but did allow them to make enough money to train and compete. If you find yourself in this situation, then a functional resume may be the best way to display your skills.

A functional resume doesn't emphasize dates and job titles. Instead, you'll be highlighting the skills that you've acquired and the functions that you've performed. This approach allows you to highlight specific work skills (such as communication, leadership, organization) and show how you acquired them through sport or through your part-time, volunteer, or short-term work experience.

The functional resume is the best approach if you are relying on your sport career to offset deficiencies in more traditional work experience.

Worksheet 9.1:
Chronological Resume Builder

Name _____

Address _____

Phone _____

Education (List the last school you attended first.)

School name _____

Location _____

Dates attended _____ to _____

Degree or program of study _____

Major and minor concentration _____

Awards or special activities _____

School name _____

Location _____

Dates attended _____ to _____

Degree or program of study _____

Major and minor concentration _____

Awards or special activities _____

School name _____

Location _____

Dates attended _____ to _____

Degree or program of study _____

Major and minor concentration _____

Awards or special activities _____

Work experience (List most recent job first.)

Company name _____

Address _____

Dates employed _____ to _____

Position title _____

Job responsibilities _____

Company name _____

Address _____

Dates employed _____ to _____

Position title _____

Job responsibilities _____

Company name _____

Address _____

Dates employed _____ to _____

Position title _____

Job responsibilities _____

Company name _____

Address _____

Dates employed _____ to _____

Position title _____

Job responsibilities _____

Other experiences (List relevant volunteer work, athletic experiences, hobbies, etc.)

_____

_____

_____

_____

Awards or honors (List any athletic, academic, or community awards or honors that you have received.)

_____

_____

_____

List the names of three people who could write a letter of reference for you.

Name _____

Address _____

Phone _____

Name _____

Address _____

Phone _____

Name _____

Address _____

Phone _____

Phone _____

You would begin to develop a functional resume by identifying the skills you acquired through sport that you believe would qualify you for the position in question. You would list several of these skills and demonstrate how you learned them. You can see how you might do this by examining the sample functional resume in highlight box 9.2.

Highlight Box 9.2

Sample Functional Resume

DONALD JONAS
92 Winter Street
Warwick, NY 08888
455-555-1111

EDUCATION

Adrion College. Richford, ID, 1994
Bachelor of Science. Business Management
GPA 3.25/4.0

Idaho State University. Summers, 1994-1995
Nine graduate credits toward MBA

SKILLS

Communications
- Team spokesperson and athlete representative for U.S. Olympic Judo Team.
- Member of Olympic Training Center Resident Athlete Planning Committee.
- Sports editor for college newspaper.
- Four courses in communications in business and industry.
- Internship in college Public Relations Office.

Organization
- Managed national judo team's travel and budget for five years.
- Maintained a high GPA while training 25 hours per week for U.S. Judo Team.
- Developed goal-setting program for junior national judo athletes.
- Codirector of summer judo camp training program.

Leadership
- Supervised a staff of 24 counselors at judo camp.
- Served as residence hall director at Olympic Training Center.
- Leadership training internship at Air Force Academy.
- Nine courses in management and leadership.

WORK HISTORY

Team captain/manager, U.S. Olympic Judo Team

Athlete representative, U.S. Olympic Committee

Self-employed painter, Jonas Painting

AWARDS

1994 National Championships, Gold Medalist in Judo
Selected to compete at two Olympic Games
U.S. Judo Federation Comeback Award, 1992

We've designed worksheet 9.2 to assist you in identifying and organizing information necessary to develop a functional resume. Before you begin, you may find it helpful to review the content, adaptive, and transferable skills that you identified in chapter 5. These skills will form the core content areas of your functional resume. You may want to fill in more than one of these worksheets if you're looking at several different types of jobs.

You may find that a resume that combines the chronological format with the functional format works best for you.

Targeted Resume

The targeted resume may be the best choice if you know the specific job that you want and believe that you have the skills to do it, even if you lack the specific training, education, or work experiences outlined in the job description. In this approach, you would emphasize how your skills and achievements qualify you for the position and how this position fits into your career development plan.

Unlike the chronological or functional resume, the targeted approach requires that you create a specific resume for each position for which you are applying. Each targeted resume requires extensive research on the company or organization and the specific position. Because you may be lacking particular qualifications, you must ensure that the person able to offer you employment reads your resume, not someone who has been assigned the task of screening applicants' resumes for basic qualifications.

Worksheet 9.2:

Functional Resume Builder

Imagine that you're writing a functional resume for a specific job. Select some of the skills that you identified during your self-exploration. List these skills and a brief description demonstrating your experience using the skill. Fill in the following outline and you'll be well on your way to developing your resume.

Career objective: _____

_____

_____

Education: _____

_____

_____

Related skills:

Skill 1 _____

   Experience using skill 1

_____

_____

Skill 2 _____

   Experience using skill 2

_____

_____

Skill 3 _____

   Experience using skill 3

_____

_____

Work experience _____

_____

_____

_____

Personal interests (including awards) _____

_____

_____

_____

_____

_____

List the names of people who will review your resume.

Reviewer 1 _____

Reviewer 2 _____

Reviewer 3 _____

The targeted approach requires substantial research effort on your part and reliance on your career network to get you the contacts and information that you need. We've provided a sample targeted resume in highlight box 9.3.

You'll notice that the job objective in a targeted resume is very specific. You are trying to communicate to a potential employer that this is the perfect job to meet the requirements of your career development strategy. To prove it, you need to promote yourself as a competent person who has the right stuff to be successful in this position. You are selling yourself, not the jobs or training that you've had. Keep this in mind as you complete worksheet 9.3. This information will form the basis for your targeted resume.

Selecting a Resume Type

The resume-building activities that you completed in worksheets 9.1, 9.2, and 9.3 helped you organize information about yourself in several formats. Now you need to examine each format and get comments from members of your support team and your career network. This will allow you to select the type of resume that meets your needs.

YOUR COVER LETTER

Unless you hand your resume directly to an employer, you should always send a cover letter with it when you are applying for a job. This letter

Sample Targeted Resume

ROBERT SMITH
U.S. Olympic Training Center
1776 East Boulder Street
Colorado Springs, CO 80909
719-111-2222

OBJECTIVE

Management trainee position, utilizing my background in business and communications, with the opportunity to demonstrate high-level motivation to succeed.

EDUCATION

B.A. in Business Administration, Management, 1992. University of Colorado, Colorado Springs.

CAPABILITIES

- Able to tactfully handle delicate communications issues and tasks.
- Able to identify and articulate the ideals of a large diversified group.
- Demonstrated high-level skill in problem solving.
- Generated new and creative ideas for team development.
- Directed work flow to ensure optimum efficiency.
- Developed high-level skills in problem solving and goal setting through sport experience.

ACHIEVEMENTS

- Maintained a high GPA while training 25 hours per week.
- Selected as athlete representative to the U.S. Olympic Committee's Long Range Planning Task Force to articulate priority needs and concerns of permanent resident athletes.
- Testified before Education Sub-Committee of the State House of Representatives in favor of in-state tuition for OTC resident athletes.
- Developed a self-monitored award program for judo team to boost team morale.

- Managed a paint contracting business with 12 part-time employees.
- Managed the U.S. National Judo Team's budget.
- Progressed from #14 to #1 in national ranking in the 78 kg division of judo.

WORK HISTORY

TEAM MANAGER/CAPTAIN Colorado Springs, CO	U.S. National Judo Team 1989, 1991
ATHLETE REPRESENTATIVE Long Range Planning Task Force	U.S. Olympic Committee August 1991
ATHLETE SPOKESPERSON Denver, CO	State House Education Sub-Committee Spring 1990
SELF-EMPLOYED CONTRACTOR Colorado Springs, CO	Smith Painting Summers 1989-1994
PERSONAL INTERESTS	Training for the 1996 Olympic Games.
REFERENCES	Available upon request.

should explain why you are writing to the employer and why you feel the employer should consider you for the position. The letter should be upbeat and should highlight one or two accomplishments that you want the employer to focus on while examining your job credentials. You might also include a significant achievement from your sport history if you feel that it might improve your chances of getting an interview.

A cover letter generally has three main sections. The opening paragraph states your intention to apply for a specific position and indicates how you learned about the opening. Be certain to give the exact job title and be specific about how you learned about the position. For example, Mary Jones, a person in your career network, told you about a job opening and encouraged you to apply. You ask Mary for permission to include her name in your cover letter. Your opening sentence might read "Please accept this letter as my application for the position of Assistant to the New England Regional Sales Manager. I learned about the position from Ms.

Worksheet 9.3:

Targeted Resume Builder

Select a specific job that interests you. Carefully review the job description and identify the qualifications and skills that the employer is seeking. Review your lists of content, adaptive, and transferable skills that you developed through sport or other work experiences. Describe any matching skills in the capabilities section. Show how you acquired that skill in the achievements section.

Objective (Match this to the position as closely as possible.)

_____

_____

_____

Education (List the last school you attended first.)

School name _____

Location _____

Dates attended _____ to _____

Degree or program of study _____

Major and minor concentration _____

Awards or special activities _____

School name _____

Location _____

Dates attended _____ to _____

Degree or program of study _____

Major and minor concentration _____

Awards or special activities _____

School name _____

Location _____

Dates attended _____ to _____

Degree or program of study _____

Major and minor concentration _____

Awards or special activities _____

Capabilities (Describe skills that match those outlined in job description.)

1. _____
2. _____
3. _____
4. _____
5. _____
6. _____
7. _____

Achievements (Describe how you acquired the skills you identified above.)

1. _____
2. _____
3. _____
4. _____
5. _____
6. _____
7. _____

Experience (List your job title and place of employment for any relevant work or volunteer experiences.)

Job title _____

Place of employment _____

Job title _____

Place of employment _____

Job title _____

Place of employment _____

Job title _____

Place of employment _____

Awards or honors (List any athletic, academic, or community awards or honors that you have received.)

_____

Mary Jones from your Detroit office and it is upon her recommendation that I am applying."

The second part of your cover letter should be a paragraph or two in which you describe why you believe you are a good match for the position and why you would like to work for that company or organization. You should highlight several specific educational, athletic, or work experiences from your resume that match the requirements outlined in the job description or otherwise show that you have the talents to make a significant contribution to the organization.

The final part of your cover letter should thank the employer for considering your application, refer the employer to your resume, and indicate how the employer can reach you or how you'll follow up with the employer. If you know that the position in question requires someone who is assertive, you could be more assertive in your closing by making a statement such as "I will call your office on Friday to schedule an interview." If you want to take a less assertive approach, you could make a statement, such as "I would be happy to discuss my interest in the position in more depth at your earliest convenience." We've provided a sample cover letter in highlight box 9.4.

Now it's time for you to practice creating your own cover letter. Select a specific job for which you are interested in applying. If you don't have a specific job in mind, choose one from your local paper's want ads or from your school's job openings list. Use the information from the job listing and your resume to complete worksheet 9.4.

After completing the exercise to build your cover letter, you know what types of information go into a cover letter and how to organize it. Remember, each cover letter should be on high-grade paper or letterhead and contain your original signature. Your goal is to present yourself professionally. Grammar and spelling errors will tell employers that you may not be as conscientious in your work as you were in your sport. Give as much time to perfecting your job search writing skills as you did to perfecting your sport.

Again, make sure that you and someone else proofread your letter before you send it out to an employer. Taking time to get advice about your resume and cover letter will ensure that you are presenting yourself in the best light. If you are successful in developing an effective resume and cover letter, you'll graduate to the next stage of the job acquisition process—the job interview.

CHAPTER SUMMARY

In this chapter, you've learned how to develop the primary written job search tools—the resume and cover letter. Although these are critical

Highlight Box 9.4

Sample Cover Letter

Maura Conant
12 Henry St.
Holland, NY, 02222
(201) 555-1234
November 20, 1996

Ms. Donna M. McCormick
Director of Personnel
American Sporting Goods Company
23 West End Ave.
Chicago, Illinois 60646

Dear Ms. McCormick:

Please accept this letter as my application for the position of marketing representative at American Sporting Goods Company. I learned of the position from Mary Smith, Director of the United States Olympic Committee's Jobs Opportunity Program.

As you will notice in my resume, I have experience not only in contacting potential contributors to the USOC, but also in conducting public relations and marketing campaigns for the Hawley Figure Skating Association. Both of these experiences have given me marketing and promotional skills that would be essential in the marketing representative position at American Sporting Goods Company.

I believe that I have the educational background, sport experience, and business skills to make a strong contribution to your company. I would appreciate an opportunity to meet with you at your convenience to discuss my qualifications more fully. I may be reached at (201) 555-9999 during most weekday hours or at (201) 555-1234 evenings.

Sincerely,
(signature)

Maura Conant
MC/
enclosure

Worksheet 9.4:
Cover Letter Builder

Your address _____

Phone _____

Date _____

Employer's name _____

Employer's title _____

Company name _____

Address _____

Dear Dr./Mr./Mrs./Ms. _____:

Opening: (Include job title and how you learned about the position.)

_____

_____

_____

_____

_____

_____

_____

Matching section: (This can be one or two paragraphs. Explain why you're a good match for the position; use specific examples; highlight several areas of your resume.)

_____

_____

_____

_____

_____

_____

_____

———————————————————————————

———————————————————————————

———————————————————————————

———————————————————————————

———————————————————————————

———————————————————————————

———————————————————————————

Closing: (State how to get in touch with you to set up an interview; remember to include your phone number[s] here as well as above.)

———————————————————————————

———————————————————————————

———————————————————————————

———————————————————————————

———————————————————————————

———————————————————————————

———————————————————————————

Sincerely,

Your name

———————————————————————————

tools in the job search, they won't by themselves get you a job. On the other hand, if you don't develop these tools, you may never land a job. Remember, a messy, cluttered, or error-filled resume or cover letter will most likely lead to your early elimination from an applicant pool. Polished resumes and cover letters can get you a job interview.

From this chapter, you should have learned the following:

1. You can use one or more of three types of resumes: chronological, functional, or targeted.
2. Employers evaluate resumes and cover letters on both content and visual display.

3. Your work history, educational background, training, and athletic experience will often dictate which type of resume is best for you.

4. Cover letters tell employers why you want a specific job and why you believe that you are qualified to get it.

Chapter
10

Interviewing and Winning the Job Offer

Now that you know how to locate job openings and write effective resumes and cover letters, you're ready to explore the final component of the job acquisition process—the job interview. No matter how well you've done to this point, you won't land the job you're seeking if you aren't successful in your interview. In this chapter, we'll help you understand the interview process and show you how to use your sport experience to prepare for and be successful in the interview game. We call it a game because we want you to view a job interview as an important contest or competition. You need to prepare yourself for the event by researching the company or organization to which you're applying and by practicing your interviewing skills.

UNDERSTANDING THE INTERVIEW PROCESS

A job interview is the normal method by which companies or organizations select new employees. It's also your opportunity to investigate how well the position and setting match your "must list" of interests, needs, and skills. During a job interview you have a chance to convince an employer that you have the skills, interests, and work habits necessary to make a solid contribution to his or her company or organization. To accomplish this, you need to present yourself in a positive light while giving an employer a chance to learn things about you that you couldn't easily put into writing.

While the employer is exploring to see if you're the right person for the position, you should be exploring whether the job is right for you. That means you should be prepared to ask questions of the employer. You should already know something about the organization or company through your job search and through the preparation of your position scouting reports in chapter 8. During the interview, you need to continue this information-gathering process to help you make a good decision. Some questions to think about while you go through the interview process include the following:

1. Is this position a good match for my most important work values, interests, and skills?

2. Would I enjoy working in this setting?

3. How does this job fit into my career plan? Will I have opportunities for promotion? Will this job help me get the experience I need to continue on the path to my ultimate career goal?

4. Does the company or organization have a solid track record for developing employees? Will it provide me with training, education, or in-service experiences to continue my development? Do they have a succession planning program that would help prepare me for other positions within the organization?

5. Will I feel valued? Do other employees feel valued?

6. Will the position provide me with enough money, benefits (such as medical and dental insurance, retirement plan, sick leave, vacations, tuition reimbursement), and free time to enjoy the lifestyle that I want? (This might include training and competing in your sport.)

As you can see, to make a good decision about your match for the position, you need to learn a lot about what the organization does and how it does it. On the other hand, the organization needs to learn about what you can do and how you might act in the position. The organization chooses how it goes about interviewing candidates for jobs; you need to know how interviews work.

Types of Interviews

Employers may conduct job interviews for different purposes and may use different formats. The simplest form of interview is a single meeting during which a job seeker and an employer exchange questions and information. If a match exists between the needs of the employer and the needs of the individual, the employer may make a job offer. On the other hand, the job interview process can be quite complex. For example, the employer might conduct a screening interview in which an administrative assistant verifies that you have the basic qualifications necessary for the position.

If you get by the screening interview, the employer would invite you back to interview with one or several people within the organization. This could be a series of one-to-one interviews or a group interview with several supervisors. These interviews may be either structured or unstructured. If you get by this stage, the employer might ask you to take a series of tests that measure your work skills and style. Some organizations may then ask you to have a final interview with the person who is in a position to hire you.

As you can see, employers may use several types of interviews. Let's examine these types in more depth so you can better prepare yourself to meet with employers.

Screening or Hiring Interview

The ultimate goal of a job interview is a job offer. If this is the goal, then your first task is to interview with the person or persons who are in a position to hire you. If an organization contacts you to come for a job interview, you should find out with whom you'll be meeting, the purpose of the meeting, and what you should bring with you. This information will help you determine whether your interview is a screening interview or a hiring interview.

Employers use screening interviews to determine whether you have the basic qualifications to do the job. Administrative assistants usually conduct such interviews. Their major responsibility is to eliminate applicants who don't have the necessary job qualifications. These persons typically ask structured questions and verify information contained in your resume. Unfortunately, administrative assistants can't offer you a job, but they can keep you from progressing to an interview with the hiring person.

If you lack the required years of experience or other specific qualifications of a position, you should try to bypass the screening interview and get directly to the hiring person. If this isn't possible, then you need to be prepared to justify how your transferable skills or nonemployment experience compensates for your lack of the specific job qualifications. You may need to convince the screening person that sport was your first career and that the skills, attitudes, and work habits you developed in sport count toward your qualifications. You've already prepared your rationale for this approach when you developed your functional resume.

Structured or Unstructured Interviews

During the interview, you should promote your special skills and ask questions of the employer to ensure that the job is a good match for your values, interests, and skills. Although this may seem like an easy task, you may have to use different strategies to accomplish these goals, depending on the format of the interview.

Interviews can be very structured and formal, or they can be unstructured and informal. For example, screening interviews tend to be very structured. Typically, in a screening interview, the interviewer asks each candidate the same set of questions. Candidates' responses are recorded and then compared to identify the individuals whose qualifications seem to match most closely the employer's needs. This type of interview tends to be very formal and have a specific time limitation.

In general, the more structured and formal the interview, the more assertive you need to be. In a structured interview, you'll need to identify places where you can interject your questions and comments. You can do this by adding related questions to the end of your responses or by tactfully interrupting the interviewer to request information. If you wait until the interviewer has asked every question on his or her list, you may not have enough time to ask questions or add comments.

In an unstructured interview, you'll have many more opportunities to interject your questions and comments. The interviewer will typically ask several general questions such as "What are your strengths and weaknesses?" or "What value could you add to our organization?" Follow-up questions will often emerge from your responses. For example, if you were describing your strengths and mentioned the leadership skills you acquired while serving as the captain of your college sports team, an interviewer might then ask, "How will that experience make you an effective supervisor?" The open style of questioning more typical of the unstructured interview will give you many opportunities to lead the conversation into areas that you want to highlight.

For both structured and unstructured situations, you should prepare your questions and practice your responses in advance. You can use two general types of questions, open and closed. Use open questions, usually beginning with words such as how and what, to get broad information (e.g., How does the company help employees continue their growth within the company?). Closed questions usually begin with words such as do or did. Use these questions to get specific information (e.g., Do you have a dental benefit plan?).

When answering open questions you'll have greater freedom in how you respond and what information you provide. This will give you more opportunities to let the interviewer know about your specific skills and work characteristics. On the other hand, if you find yourself faced with a series of closed questions, you'll need to learn how to respond to the closed question as if it were an open question. For example, if you were asked, "Do you have two years of supervisory experience?" you could mentally change the question to "What kinds of supervisory experience do you have?" This skill is particularly useful in screening interviews when you lack specific qualifications outlined in the job description but have appropriate transferable skills. Practicing responses to different types of questions is a major part of preparing for the content component of the interview.

Managing the Job Interview

Although interviews can take many different forms and styles, all interviews have three common phases—an opening, a two-way matching process between employer and applicant, and a closing. You need to be prepared to present and conduct yourself well in each of these phases. Just as your resumes and cover letters were evaluated on appearance and content, so will you be. Let's begin by looking at the three parts of an interview.

Every interview begins with an opening phase when you'll meet the interviewer, exchange greetings, and get ready to begin. Often, you and the interviewer will briefly exchange information unrelated to the position. The interviewer may ask about the weather, directions, or driving conditions. This casual communication is your first opportunity to score a few points with the interviewer.

During the opening, you want to listen intently and make the situation as comfortable as you can. Remember, some interviewers may feel awkward during this phase of the interview, too. If you can put them (and yourself) at ease by carrying on the conversation, you'll be off to a good start. Using open questions and listening well are your best tools in building a comfortable relationship. However, you don't want to carry this casual conversation too far. A good rule of thumb is to take your lead from the interviewer.

Although the opening phase may be brief, first impressions can be quite powerful factors in the interview process. Later in the chapter, we'll provide you with specific tips on how to present yourself, but recognize that employers will judge you on both how you present yourself and what you say.

The middle phase of the interview focuses on job content and qualifications. At this point, you're trying to determine if the position is right for you, and the employer is trying to determine if you're right for the position.

Earlier in this chapter, we outlined some questions for you to think about as you evaluate your compatibility with a position. During the middle phase of the interview, you should be prepared to ask questions about the typical tasks and duties of the position to help you in estimating your fit with the organization. Questions such as "What would be the scope of my responsibilities?" and "How much supervision can I expect to receive?" show your interest in the organization and help you evaluate the position. Later in this chapter, we'll provide you with a list of questions that employers typically ask job candidates.

The final part of the interview is the closing. You should thank the interviewer or interviewers for giving you the opportunity to speak with them. You can briefly share what impressed you about the company and reaffirm your interest in the position. It's important to ask about the next step in the hiring process and when you might expect to hear back from the company. Be social, but don't overstay your welcome.

Presenting Yourself

During the interview, you should pay attention to your behavior and appearance. You want to present yourself in a manner that would lead an employer to want to get to know you better. Some tips to accomplish this include the following:

1. Pay attention to your physical behavior as you would during a sporting event. Control your body movements so that nervous habits don't distract the employer.

2. Maintain eye contact and smile at appropriate times. Employers want to know that you can relate well to customers, clients, and other employees.

3. Use your nervous energy to show enthusiasm. If you feel excessively nervous, use some of the relaxation techniques you may have learned from your sport.

4. Dress in a style appropriate to the position for which you're applying. Wear clothing that you would wear if you were representing the company or institution on the road. Coaches, for example, usually wear suits or jackets to competitions.

   If you're in doubt about what to wear, ask people in the field what is suitable. An interview isn't the time to make a statement about your individuality.

5. Grooming and neatness are extremely important. Sloppy appearance suggests sloppy work habits.

6. Use your words and your voice to make an impression of being confident. A quiet voice and hesitancy can indicate a lack of confidence, while using slang and loudness may suggest rudeness or cockiness. A videotape session of a mock interview can help you see and hear yourself in action, the same way that videos helped you evaluate yourself in sport.

Preparing for Questions

Now that you've considered how to present yourself, it's time to examine and prepare the content of the interview. One of the best ways to do this is to prepare yourself for the questions the interviewer might ask. You can practice ahead of time with a friend or a person in your support network. Highlight box 10.1 contains some possible questions that an employer might ask.

Highlight Box 10.1

Sample Interview Questions

1. What are your long-term career goals?
2. Why are you interested in this particular job opening?
3. What are your strengths and weaknesses?
4. How has your education helped you in preparing for this job?

5. How would you describe yourself?

6. Why should I hire you for this position?

7. Why are you interested in our company or organization?

8. Are you willing to relocate?

9. In this particular job, what would be your greatest challenges?

10. How do you work under pressure?

11. In what ways do you think you might make a special contribution to our company?

12. What type of a team player are you?

13. What have you learned from your mistakes?

14. Do you plan to continue your education?

15. Describe your most rewarding experience.

16. Would it be hard for you to start at the bottom of our company after you have been on the top in your athletic career?

17. Where do you expect to be working and what do you expect to be earning five years from now?

18. In what type of environment would you prefer to work?

19. What is your leadership style?

20. What questions do you have for me about the position or the company?

After going through the question list, you may have noticed that some questions were more difficult to respond to than others. You should make notes about how you might answer these difficult questions and plan your responses. Just thinking about your responses is helpful, but it's not enough. You wouldn't just think about what you need to do to be successful in a major competition. You would practice. Do the same for the interview situation. Give the list of sample interview questions to members of your support team and have them take you through practice interviews. This kind of preparation will help polish both your responses to interview questions and the way you present yourself.

Evaluating Your Interview Performance

Recall that we first described the interview as a game or competition. We did that to help you see the parallels between preparing for a competition and preparing for a job interview. Did you ever get to a point in your sport career where you stopped practicing because you felt your performance was perfect? We would guess that you're having trouble even thinking about that question. Well, we want you to approach the interview game in the same way.

After each practice or actual interview we want you to evaluate how you did. Remember, you may have performed very well in a competition but not won the event. It's the same way in an interview; you may have done well but failed to land the job offer. That's why you want to evaluate the interview to see which parts went well and which areas need improvement. Worksheet 10.1 contains some questions that will help you evaluate your interview skills.

Worksheet 10.1:
Interview Evaluation Form

Check whether this is a practice interview or an actual job interview.

Practice _____   Date _____

(If practice, have an observer complete this form.)

Job interview _____   Date _____

Position _____

Company _____

A. Use the following scale to evaluate your performance.

Excellent (You came across very well.) = 3
Adequate (You did OK, but you need improvement.) = 2
Poor (You felt uncomfortable and need a lot of practice.) = 1

  1. *Presenting yourself*

  _____ I appeared to be dressed appropriately.

  _____ I made appropriate eye contact.

  _____ I spoke in a clear and direct manner.

  _____ I was in control of my nervous energy.

  _____ I smiled at appropriate times.

_____ I appeared enthusiastic.

_____ I spoke in a confident manner.

2. *Responding to questions*

_____ I felt comfortable with my responses.

_____ I answered each question clearly and directly.

_____ I responded to closed questions as if they were open questions.

_____ I felt prepared for questions.

_____ **Total**

B. List any questions that you felt under-prepared to answer.

_____

_____

_____

_____

_____

_____

_____

C. List any aspects of your interview performance that you need to improve. If you're having problems with specific situations (e.g., controlling your nervous energy), use your goal-setting strategy to plan your course of action.

_____

_____

_____

_____

_____

_____

_____

After each interview, remember to send a letter to the interviewer thanking him or her and other staff members for taking the time to interview with you. Reaffirm your interest in the position and indicate how you plan to follow up on the interview to determine your status in the decision process.

ACCEPTING THE OFFER

If you prepared yourself well and if you're a good match for a position, you may receive a job offer. That's the good news. Now, you face the sometimes difficult decision of whether or not to accept an offer. If you've done your homework, you have enough information to know if this is the right job for you. Unfortunately, the decision to accept a job, like all decisions, involves some degree of risk. By choosing one job, you may be giving up other possibilities. Should you wait for a better offer? Is a bird in the hand better than two in the bush? Only you can decide, but doing research and using your support network can facilitate your decision-making process.

When you get an offer, confirm all the specific information that was discussed during the interview, including salary, benefits, and extras (e.g., travel expenses, relocation assistance, profit sharing). Calculate all of these items when considering your total compensation. In addition, you need to determine a starting date.

Remember, you know how to get the information that you need to help you decide whether to accept or reject a job offer. Good information leads to the best decisions.

CHAPTER SUMMARY

Well, there you have it. You've now learned the final skills necessary to be successful in the career search. With a lot of preparation and a little luck, you'll have a successful campaign.

In this chapter, you should have learned the following:

1. Employers may use several types and formats of job interviews.
2. Interviews are two-way streets in which you explore if a particular job is right for you, while the employer explores if you're right for the job.

3. In preparing for interviews, you should know how to present yourself as well as what to say about yourself.

4. Evaluating job interview performance can help you prepare for future interviews.

Some Final Thoughts

Congratulations. You've spent some time working on a very important project—you. The more you know about yourself and the options available to you, the better choices you'll probably make. In the introduction to this book, we suggested that luck was "when preparation meets opportunity." Well, if you've completed the exercises in this book, you should be prepared to take advantage of any career opportunities that present themselves.

Remember that the career-planning skills you've learned can help you in other aspects of your life. In fact, many of the skills that you learned through sport are transferable and will help you manage life decisions and transitions that you'll face in future years. No matter where you are in your sport or postsport life cycle, you can use these skills to help you be successful and reach your goals.

It's never too late or too early to start planning for the future. One athlete told us this:

> Giving up sport and finding out where you fit in society is not very easy, but it's nice to know that there are people out there who care and who can help out. At first, I thought getting a job was sending resumes to want ads. Now I know how to get the job that I really want. It really helped to realize that the time I spent competing was not a waste and that I did learn many skills that will help me be successful in my next career.

Like the athletes you read about in this book, you have many skills to offer. The more you know about yourself and your resources, the smoother your life transitions are likely to be. By completing this book, you've jump-started your planning for the future. Go for your goals and realize your dreams. We wish you much success.

Appendix
A

Additional Career Resources

Careers in Sports

Careers for Sports Nuts and Other Athletic Types
    By W. Heitzmann

Developing a Career in Sport
    By Greg Cylkowski

Athlete's Game Plan for College and Career
    By Howard and Stephen Figler

Career Opportunities in the Sports Industry
    By S. Field

College Guides

College Majors and Careers: A Resource Guide for Effective Life Planning
   By P. Phifer

Guide to American Colleges
   By Melissa Cass and Julia Cass-Liepmann

Peterson's Annual Guide
   By Peterson's Guides

General Occupational Information

Career Choices for the 90's
   Walker Publishing

Emerging Careers: New Occupations for the Year 2000
   Garrett Park Press

Careers Encyclopedia
   VGM Career Horizons

The Enhanced GOE: Descriptions for the 2500 Most Important Jobs
   JIST Works Inc.

General Self-Assessment and Job Search Guides

What Color is Your Parachute?
   By Richard Bolles

Knock 'Em Dead
   By Martin Yate

Perfect Job Search
   By Tom Jackson

Joy of Not Working
   By Ernie Zelinski

Do What You Love, the Money Will Follow
   By Marsha Sinetar

Do What You Are
   By Paul Tieger

Working Harder Isn't Working
   By Bruce O'Hara

Guerilla Tactics in the Job Market
By Tom Jackson

Skills for Success: A Guide to the Top for Men and Women
By Adele Steele

Job Search Guides for College Graduates

The Berkeley Guide to Employment for New College Graduates
By James Briggs

Real World 101, What College Never Taught You About Success
By James Calano and Jeff Saltzman

Student's Guide to Finding a Superior Job
By William Cohen

Annual Guide to Career Planning, Job Search, and Work-Related Education
By College Placement Council

Peterson's Annual Guide
By Peterson's Guides

Resume-Writing and Interview Skills

Perfect Resume Strategies
By Tom Jackson

Resume Kit
By Richard Beatty

Damn Good Resume Guide
By Yana Parker

How to Write Better Resumes
By Adele Lewis

Resumes That Get Jobs: How to Write Your Best Resume
Arco Publishing

High Impact Interview
By Jeff Staller

Sweaty Palms: The Neglected Art of Being Interviewed
By Anthony Medley

Specific Career Information

Careers in Science
    by VGM Career Horizons

Careers in Health and Fitness
    By J. Heron

VGM Opportunity Series
    by VGM Career Horizons

Appendix
B

Sport-Related Careers

Academic Athletic Advisor

- Advise athletes on course selection, time management, goal setting, and concerns related to sport eligibility
- May do some sport-related and non-sport-related counseling, as well as some performance enhancement

Athletic Counselor

- Counsel athletes on issues such as career termination and transferable skills, as well as non-sport-related issues
- May do some performance enhancement with athletes

Athletic Director

- Supervise, develop, and administer a school's athletic programs and sports department
- Organize and supervise physical educators and coaches

Athletic Equipment Designer

- Create or design equipment for athletes
- Make the equipment more useful, easier to use, and more effective

Athletic Fashion Designer

- Create styles of clothing for elite athletes or the general public

Athletic Trainer

- Design and implement injury prevention and rehabilitation programs
- Provide immediate treatment of current injuries
- Travel with the team and attend all practices and competitions

Camp Manager

- Supervise and recruit camp counselors
- Plan and direct camp activities
- Work with children and young adults

Coaching

- Train and motivate athletes to perform competitively
- Recruit athletes, develop lineup and competition strategies
- Can coach a team or an individual athlete

Director of College Intramural Programs

- Organize and advertise availability of sports for fun for men and women college students
- Organize competitions, officials, scoring, and tournament results

Health/Fitness Trainer

- Train others to organize fitness programs and evaluate programs
- Educate individuals about health and fitness

Landscape Architect for Athletic Areas

- Design and supervise the building of athletic stadiums, fields, buildings, and recreational areas

Outdoor Leadership Program Trainer

- Supervise program leaders or instructors
- Develop and direct training programs for instructors
- Supervise and evaluate programs

Personal Trainer

- Provide exercise and fitness programs for individuals' best fitness level

Physical Education

- Instruct sport-related classes and evaluate students
- Adhere to mandated physical education and fitness requirements

Physical Therapist

- Work with athletes who have been injured to restore function, reduce pain, prevent more injuries, and get athletes competing again quickly
- Usually athletes will have been referred by a physician who has prescribed a rehabilitation treatment program

Professional Athlete

- Master and continually practice and develop skills in sport
- Compete in sport as a career and make a living at sport

Publications Writer

- Develop press releases and produce other sport-related media
- Create positive images for athletes and athletics through publications

Radio Sportscaster

- Report sport-related news to radio audiences
- Provide color commentary during competitions

Recreation Facilities Director

- Organize and supervise planning for recreation programs, budget, and employees

Recreation Therapist

- Organize and supervise recreational activities
- Prescribe recreational activities for individuals

Resort/Park/Health Club Management

- Organize and supervise fitness services, activities, and events
- Hire employees; manage the organization's budget

Sport Psychologist

- Employ performance enhancement techniques that pertain to mental toughness, coping, concentration, and "psyching"
- Generally trained in both physical education and psychology

Sport and Recreation Facilities Planner

- Develop, supervise, and evaluate programs for sport and recreation
- Hire and train instructors for programs

Sports Advertisement Designer

- Create and "sell" advertisements for a sporting event or team

Sport Biologist

- Have knowledge of the physiology of exercise—what happens with the body during sport and exercise
- Teach or do research in the area of movement science and sport biology

Sport Historian

- Study the history of sport and sport-related areas
- Publish works on history of sport

Sports Illustrator

- Create images of sports through art

Sports Information Director

- Provide sport-related information to the public
- Promote ticket sales and the reputation of the team through articles, interviews, press announcements, and other materials

Sports Journalist

- Report sport-related information through articles and feature stories
- Attend sport competitions and other sport-related events

Sports Marketing Executive

- Create advertisements, promotions, and fund-raising plans to create income for costly sports
- Design marketing plans to measure the need and interest for sports facilities

Sports Medicine

- Deal with treatment and rehabilitation of injured athletes as well as injury prevention
- Sports medicine professionals include sports physicians, ortho-pedists, chiropractors, physical therapists, athletic trainers, and massage therapists

Sport Nutritionist

- Consult with teams or individual athletes to develop beneficial diets
- Knowledge in weight control, vitamins, and precompetition meals may help prevent injury and maintain athletes' health

Sports Official

- In-depth knowledge of the sport
- Constant education, training, or certification to keep up on current rules and regulations of the sport

Sports Photographer

- Take photos of sport-related events and participants

Sport Physiologist

- Study and analyze improvement of athletes' endurance, muscle strength, and flexibility
- Evaluate athletes' potential, develop conditioning and injury prevention programs, and consult with others who work with the athletes

Team Manager

- Organize and supervise the training, planning, on-field performance, and evaluation of the athletes
- Currently assuming more corporate responsibilities such as finance, promotions, and labor negotiations

Team Scout

- Travel to sporting events to evaluate athletes
- Report to coaches, owners, general managers about athletes

TV Sportscaster

- Narrate sports information to television viewers
- Edit information for sportscast; provide commentary during competitions

Index

About the Authors

Al Petitpas, EdD, is professor of psychology and director of the graduate training program in Athletic Counseling at Springfield College in Springfield, Massachusetts. He has designed and implemented career development and transition programs for elite athletes, including the Career Assistance Program for Athletes (CAPA) for the U.S. Olympic Committee (USOC) and the Planning for Future Careers Program for the Ladies Professional Golf Association (LPGA). He also helped develop the NCAA Youth Education through Sports program (YES).

Working in the area of career development for more than 20 years, **Delight E. Champagne, PhD,** has helped athletes at the college and professional level, including the USOC and LPGA. She is a professor of psychology at Springfield College where she coordinates the graduate preparation program in student personnel and teaches graduate-level career development courses.

Judy Chartrand, PhD, is a research scientist for Consulting Psychologists Press and works out of her office in Lindstrom, Minnesota. In 1995 she received the Early Career Award from the Counseling Division of the American Psychology Association for her work in career development. She has consulted with U.S. Olympic Team athletes for CAPA.

Steven J. Danish, PhD, is the director of the Life Skills Center and professor of psychology and preventative medicine at Virginia Commonwealth University in Richmond, Virginia. Dr. Danish, a licensed psychologist and a registered sport psychologist at the Sports Medicine Division of the USOC, developed the Going for the Goal program.

Throughout his career, **Shane M. Murphy, PhD,** has helped hundreds of athletes with performance and personal concerns. He served as the sport psychologist for the USOC from 1987 to 1994. Murphy is president of Gold Medal Consultants in Monroe, Connecticut, where he works with athletes, business executives, and other elite performers.

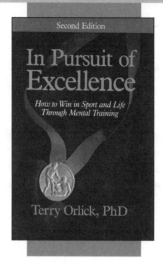
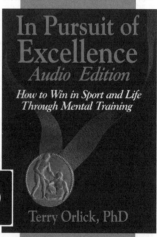